Oshun

The Ultimate Guide to an Orisha of Yoruba and Santería, the Divine Feminine, and Ifa

Your Free Gift
(only available for a limited time)

Thanks for getting this book! If you want to learn more about various spirituality topics, then join Mari Silva's community and get a free guided meditation MP3 for awakening your third eye. This guided meditation mp3 is designed to open and strengthen ones third eye so you can experience a higher state of consciousness. Simply visit the link below the image to get started.

https://spiritualityspot.com/meditation

Table of Contents

Introduction

Oshun is among the most powerful female deities in Yoruba, Santeria, and Ifa. She is one of the 401 Orishas created by the supreme deity Oludumare, and she acts as a messenger between this powerful being and people. Often called the *divine feminine,* Oshun is a benevolent goddess who looks out for those under her patronage. Even though it's mainly women who tend to adopt her as their patron, she can be revered by anyone who wishes to form a connection with her. Her main powers include bringing love and prosperity to her followers, and she is also associated with running water and fertility. At the beginning of this book, you'll learn about her different aspects as viewed by the ancient Yoruba religion, *Ifa,* and the African Diaspora religion, *Santeria.*

According to Yoruba lore, all people hail from the Orishas. Bearing this in mind, everyone has at least one parent, Orisha. In this book, you'll learn to identify your parent Orisha and discover whether you're Oshun's child. After that, you'll be introduced to the colorful legends, myths, and stories (*patakis*) connected to Oshun, including her ever-popular love story with Shango and stories involving her mother, Yemaya, and son, Eshu. Learning about her interactions with the other Orishas and humans will help you understand how to connect to her divine feminine essence. While she is only the archetype of this power, her stories have much to tell about the connection between the divine feminine and the divine masculine.

The subsequent chapters will be a comprehensive guide to Oshun's symbolism. You'll be introduced to her favorite plants, offerings, and the associations you can use to honor her, connect with her, and ask her for favors and blessings. One of the best ways to celebrate her is to visit her favorite places. These are rivers, waterfalls, and other sources of sweet water. Another excellent way to venerate any deity, including Oshun, is to build an altar. The book will give you all the information you need to create and dedicate this sacred space to the goddess. While having a dedicated altar is unnecessary, it can do wonders for building your spiritual connection with her, especially if you're her child.

Once you've learned about her association, you'll be ready to expand your knowledge of the spells and rituals you can perform to honor her. You'll also be able to use these to communicate with her and use her ashe in order to better your life. The relevant chapter offers plenty of spells and rituals and spells for love, beauty, abundance, and prosperity, along with beginner-friendly instructions for each work. You'll be able to perform these on her holy days and festivals.

Lastly, you'll learn that you don't have to wait for a momentous occasion to venerate Oshun. The little tips and tricks provided in the last chapter can help you align with her energy on a day-to-day basis, allowing you to form a much deeper bond with her. You'll find beginner-friendly guides for meditating, crafting, and other activities. Just practicing self-love will help you connect to this divine feminine. If you're ready to embark on this journey and start celebrating Oshun, all you need to do is keep reading.

Chapter 1: Oshun - Spirit, Saint, Orisha

Oshun is among the most significant and influential Orishas in the Yoruba, Santeria, and Ifa religions. These religions originated in Africa but have managed to spread to different countries around the world. This chapter will introduce these three religions, the concept of the Orishas, Oshun, and her role in them.

An artistic depiction of the birth of Oshun.
Tmanner38, CC BY-SA 4.0 <https://creativecommons.org/licenses/by-sa/4.0>, via Wikimedia Commons https://commons.wikimedia.org/wiki/File:Birth_of_Oshun_HR.JPG.jpg

Oshun in Yoruba

The Yoruba Religion

The Yoruba religion originated in Western Africa, particularly in West Nigeria. The Yoruba people consist of various ethnic groups, and they reside in the southern Sahara desert. It is one of the oldest religions in the world, even predating Christianity. They have their own set of beliefs and traditions, which they have been practicing for years. Their religious customs are based on their culture and history, and they influenced their literature, arts, and lives, creating fascinating and rich mythology, songs, and proverbs. The Yoruba people passed down their traditions orally from one generation to the next. Therefore, one myth can have several different versions.

People from all over the world practice Yoruba – even in the U.S.; the religion found its way to the new world during the slave trade. The African people were forced to convert to Catholicism and prohibited from practicing their own beliefs. However, they still held on to their religious traditions and practiced them in private.

Olodumare is the supreme deity of the Yoruba religion and the creator of the universe. In different myths, he goes by the name Olofin or Olodumare-Olorun. Olodumare doesn't have a gender and is usually referred to as "they" because they are all things and can't be categorized into one gender. In the religious hierarchy system, Olodumare sits at the top. There is no one above the deity who existed before the universe itself.

- Olodumare
- Orishas
- Mankind
- Ancestors
- Plants and animals

The Yoruba religion doesn't have the concept of the angel or devil because they believe nothing is all good or all bad. Everything has a positive and negative side. However, there are similar beings to demons who are known as Ajoguns. They are trickster beings who, unlike the Orishas, bring misfortune to mankind.

The spirits of the ancestors also play a big role in the Yoruba religion. They are individuals who had an influence on mankind when they were alive, like brave warriors or kings. After they die, the living keep their memories alive by honoring and making offerings to them when they need their guidance.

On the bottom of the hierarchy are plants and animals. Although they don't have the same power as other beings, they are no less significant.

Ayanmo, or fate, is a main concept in Yoruba. According to its cosmology, when all humans were created, they chose their destiny, where they would be born, who they would marry, how many children they had, what they would do with their lives, and even how they would die. However, when they come to Earth, they forget their destiny and spend their lives trying to remember and achieve it. Each human being is assigned an Orisha who helps them realize their Ayanmo.

In some cases, a person can die before they achieve their destiny, but they are usually given a second chance through reincarnation. Reincarnation in the Yoruba religion is often regarded as a positive experience. It is a reward for the people who lead an honorable and virtuous life.

In the Yoruba religion, it is also believed that the soul continues to live on after death. The soul is then reincarnated into another body, where it can continue its journey toward fulfilling its destiny. This process is seen as a natural cycle of life and death, and it is believed that the soul can be reborn multiple times until it achieves its true purpose. The Yoruba people also believe that reincarnation is a way for the soul to learn valuable lessons and gain wisdom, which will help it to achieve its destiny in the next life. Ultimately, reincarnation is viewed as a journey toward spiritual enlightenment and ultimate liberation from the cycle of birth and death.

Orishas

Right after Olodumare comes the Orishas, who are the most significant beings in the Yoruba religion. Orishas or Orisas are supernatural entities and are different aspects of Olodumare. They are often described as deities, demigods, or spirits. Olodumare created the Orishas before creating the universe. The deity breathed life into all mankind which makes all humans connected to one another.

The concept of the supreme deity is too complicated for the simple human brain to comprehend, so Olodumare couldn't directly communicate with the people. The deity also lives in the heavens, far away from Earth, so they are unable to listen to people's prayers and are usually unaware of the affairs of mankind. For this reason, Olodumare created the Orishas to act as intermediaries between them and humans. The deity randomly gave each Orisha a domain of influence where they would watch and protect mankind and report to Olodumare. There is an Orisha for everything like thunder, agriculture, water, rivers, iron, hunting, and love.

However, some historians don't agree that Olodumare was a distant and unaware deity. They state that some stories portrayed Olodumare as an attentive god who was involved in the lives of mankind and heard their prayers.

Orishas are highly revered among the Yoruba people because they greatly impact their daily affairs. They interfere in every aspect of human life but only when needed. The relationship between mankind and Orishas is mutually beneficial as both cannot survive without the other. The people venerate the Orishas and present them with offerings while the Orishas, in turn, provide their assistance.

Although one can seek the help of any Orisha, modern practitioners prefer "The Seven African Powers." These seven are considered the most powerful and influential out of all these Orishas.

1. Oshun, the Orisha of love and fertility.
2. Shango, the Orisha of thunder and lighting.
3. Yemaya, the Earth mother and the mother of Orishas.
4. Esu, the messenger between the Orishas and mankind and is the trickster Orisha.
5. Obatala, the sky Orisha and creator of mankind.
6. Oya, the Orisha of death and rebirth.
7. Ogun, the Orisha of iron and metal.

Orishas aren't perfect beings. They have many human qualities, have made mistakes, and caused trouble to the supreme deity. In one story, they tried to kill Olodumare and take his place because the god was getting old. They believed that they should rule alone since they were more involved in people's lives and didn't need the deity's permission or supervision. Many stories show the Orishas as imperfect beings with egos

– who are sometimes weak when faced with their desires. However, they are still responsible beings and always come through when people call for them.

Therefore, one can't describe the Orishas as gods. They have human weaknesses, and their powers are still limited since they can't do anything without Olodumare's permission. For instance, in the creation myth, when Obatala wanted to create dry land and mankind, he first had to go to Olodumare for permission. However, they still share similarities with gods as they have powers, can hear prayers, and can help humans.

No one has ever seen an Orisha. They are depicted in several paintings based on their description in mythology and using known characteristics. Even when you invoke them, they won't appear to you. They possess a willing person, usually a priest or priestess, during certain rituals.

Orishas can sometimes cause problems for people instead of helping them. They don't do this intentionally, but they are flawed and have goals that can influence their actions. Like human beings, they struggle between their duty and their personal desires.

Oshun

After Olodumare created the universe, he felt that it was missing something. It needed love, romance, beauty, and sweetness, so he created Oshun. Oshun, which is also spelled Ochun, Osun, or Oxum, is pronounced as "O-shan," and she is the Orisha of love, beauty, freshwater, purity, sensuality, and fertility. She is described as a goddess and spirit and is the youngest of all Orishas. Some legends mention that Yemaya was her mother, while others state that she was her younger sister. Oshun is Olodumare's favorite, and she is one of the few allowed to communicate directly with the supreme deity and deliver messages to him from the Orishas.

Oshun played a huge role in creating the universe, and various myths mention how she helped save the world too. She is extremely powerful and can be either a force of destruction or a force of creativity. She is fair and doesn't enjoy the extreme actions she sometimes has to take, but she only punishes those who deserve it, like when someone disrespects nature or the divine, offends her, or shows cruelty toward other humans or creatures. She can bring drought by withholding the rain or causing floods. You should never cross Oshun as she is vindictive, and her sweet nature can instantaneously change to reveal a terrifying Orisha.

Her anger is merely a response to sinners and doesn't reflect her true character. Oshun is described as loving, kind-hearted, generous, noble, merciful, and warm. She is a symbol of feminine beauty and has domain over all types of relationships. She protects, guides, heals, and provides fertility for those who respect her and repent for their mistakes. Never has Oshun broken a promise, and she expects her followers to keep their word as well. She rewards their loyalty by always answering when they call on her.

Oshun is always there for her people and shows sympathy to those struggling or experiencing big changes in their lives and heading toward new beginnings. When someone loses a loved one and is dealing with grief, Oshun helps them deal with their pain.

Oshun has the same qualities as the rivers she rules over. She is charming and charismatic, *and many male Orishas find her irresistible.* On the outside, Oshun seems like a happy Orisha who lights every room she walks into with her beauty and positive attitude. However, deep down, she suffers and struggles with loneliness, sadness, and heartache. As the Orisha of love, she often gives her heart to those she cares about. However, no one has ever shown her the same amount of passion, love, and devotion, which is why she always ends up disappointed.

Oshun is a beautiful, sensual, seductive Orisha with a lovely feminine figure. She is depicted wearing a golden dress decorated with beautiful jewels. She often holds a mirror in her hand to marvel at her own beauty, showcasing her vanity.

Human beings first encountered Oshun in Nigeria in a town called Osogbo. To this day, the people of Yoruba consider it a sacred place. They live under her protection, and, in return, they venerate her and present offerings.

Just like all Orishas, Oshun is flawed and has human qualities and weaknesses. She was Shango's second wife. He was also married to Oba, the Orisha of time and rivers. She was jealous of Oba and played tricks to make Shango hate her. In most legends, Oshun is portrayed in a heroic light by always doing the right thing. However, the stories that show her humane and weak side makes her relatable. People identify with her as they see her as an imperfect being who also makes mistakes.

Oshun is associated with magic and is often called "the queen of witches." She teaches her followers spells and mysticism. Oshun enjoys watching people fall in love and will cast spells that bring lovers together.

People invoke Oshun when they're in need of prosperity, good luck, change, health, and strength. Although she is an Orisha for all people, she pays extra attention to women. She helps those who are looking for love or who want to get pregnant.

Oshun and the Myth of Creation

In Yoruba mythology, the Orisha Obatala played a huge role in creating the universe. When Olodumare first created the world, there was only sky and water. Obatala felt that the world was lacking, so he asked for Olodumare's permission to build and create lands which he agreed to. With the help of Orunmila and other Orishas, Obatala descended to Earth and began creating dry land. After Obatala finished, he spent some time on Earth enjoying his creation. However, he felt lonely and desired company. He asked Olodumare's permission to create human beings, and again, he obliged. However, Obatala was drunk during the creation process and ended up making deformed people. Before realizing his mistake, he asked Olodumare to breathe life into them. When Obatala woke up, he realized what he had done and was horrified. He vowed to never drink again and became the protector of the disabled.

Obatala played a huge role in creating the universe.
https://www.flickr.com/photos/fenixcsmar/34206000186

Now that the universe was created, Olodumare sent some of his Orishas to Earth to complete the process. There were sixteen male Orishas and one female, Oshun. Oshun had many ideas on how she wanted to spread beauty and love in the universe. However, because she was young and female, the other Orishas didn't listen to any of her ideas. She was offended and left. They continued their work, but without Oshun's guidance, they failed. They didn't know what to do and had no choice but to go to Olodumare and tell them that they couldn't complete their mission. Olodumare was bewildered that Oshun wasn't with them and asked about her. They told them what had happened. Olodumare was rightfully angry. Not only did they fail their mission and ignore Olodumare's orders, but they also disrespected the deity's favorite Orisha. He told them that for this mission to work, they must listen to Oshun. The male Orishas put their egos aside and apologized to Oshun. She accepted their apology and accompanied them once again to Earth. She blessed the world with love, beauty, and fertility.

Oshun in Santeria

The Santeria Religion

The Santeria religion is also called "La Religión Lucumí" which is Spanish for "The Order of Lucumí," and "La Regla de Ocha," which means "The Order of the Orishas." The word "Santeria" means saints or the way of the saints. The religion's practitioners often describe the Orishas as saints. When the Afro-Cubans arrived in the new world, they were forced to convert to Christianity. Since they wanted to keep practicing their own religious beliefs, they found a parallelism between Santeria and Catholicism, giving them a chance to practice both religions. They found that the Catholic saints and the Orishas had many things in common as they both acted as intermediaries between God and the people. They assigned Catholic saints to their Orishas, so they could appear to practice Catholicism when they were, in fact, practicing their own religion. This connection added to the complexity of Santeria. In this context, Oshun was linked to Our Lady of Mercy.

There is a misconception that the Afro-Cubans merged Santeria with Catholicism. However, it was more of a parallelism based on the similarities between the two religions. To this day, there are people who practice both religions as they don't find any contradictions between them. For instance, someone can go to church while still practicing

Santeria at their home or decorate their homes with Orisha pictures *and* statues of Catholic saints.

The Afro-Cubans practiced Santeria in secret for hundreds of years. After the Cuban revolution, the government acknowledged and accepted Santeria, and the people were allowed to freely practice their religious beliefs. However, there were still some concerns about the religion because of its association with witchcraft.

The religion originated in West Africa and was brought to countries like Brazil, Cuba, Puerto Rico, Haiti, and the U.S.A. during the slave trade. It is a diverse faith combining different beliefs from many cultures and religions, like the Yoruba religion, Catholicism, and Caribbean traditions.

Orishas

Orishas play a similar role in Santeria. They watch over mankind, report to Olodumare and assist the people when they need help. Invoking an Orisha requires rituals or divination. A priest or priestess leads a ritual and invites an Orisha to possess them. The attendees then ask for advice and guidance. Some Santeria practitioners even invoke Orishas to help them with their magical practices.

There are many similarities between Santeria and Yoruba. In both religions, Olodumare created the universe and left it to the Orishas to watch over it and provide assistance to the people. In Santeria, Orishas are also extremely powerful and can do the impossible, which is why people call on them when they are helpless. However, they also have the power to bring misfortune to mankind. When a person experiences bad luck, it usually means they have been neglecting their Orisha. Building an altar, praying, or presenting offerings can get you back on their good side. When Orisha is happy with you, you will feel better and notice an improvement in all areas of your life.

Orishas aren't immortal, and without the people's acknowledgment and offerings, they can't survive.

Oshun

Love is what makes life worth living. Olodumare realized this fact after creating the universe. The only thing that can guarantee this new world's survival is for people to experience love. Olodumare created Oshun (also spelled Ochún's) and sent her to Earth to spread love and joy among the people. Oshun is very close and devoted to her mother (or elder sister), Yemaya, and they both work together very well. Yemaya as Orisha's mother, and Oshun, as her love. Orishas help people with issues concerning love, motherhood, and marriage.

Oshun seduces men with her dancing, charming laugh, and full hips. Many Orishas and people consider Oshun to be inexperienced because of her young age. However, on more than one occasion, she has proven herself to be smarter and more capable than other Orishas. She is very good friends with Orisha's messenger Esu. She was married to multiple Orishas like Shango, Ogun, Orúnmila (the Orisha of wisdom and divination), and Ochosi (the Orisha of hunting.) She is the daughter of the creator Orisha Obatala and sister of Oya and Oba (the river Orisha). She learned a lot from her husband, Orúnmila, and became a very talented diviner as well. Although she had many husbands, she never loved anyone as much as Shango. From the moment she met him, she fell for him. However, Shango was a womanizer and broke her heart many times. Yet, he remained her greatest love.

Although she is a powerful Orisha, Oshun can act like a spoiled child and get very angry when people ignore her or don't meet her demands. She has saved human beings and other Orishas on more than one occasion. She has a domain on all types of freshwater, like ponds and lakes. All the elements necessary for life on Earth, like love, water, and prosperity, are under her control.

Oshun in Ifa

Ifa is a religion that is based on divination. It originated in Yoruba from the Olori family and is heavily influenced by magic. Ifa also focuses on venerating the spirits of the ancestors and healing. Similar to the Abrahamic religions, Ifa followers worship only one god, Olodumare.

Orishas play a prominent role in the Ifa religion, and each one of them is associated with an element of nature. Practitioners seek the Orisha's help through divination, incantation, and prayers. They can appear to people in their dreams to give advice or answer their questions.

Oshun's role in Ifa is similar to her role in Yoruba and Santeria. She provides guidance and assistance but must be respected, or she will exert vengeance on those who offend her. As an expert diviner, Oshun greatly impacts the Ifa religion.

Yoruba, Santeria, and Ifa share many things in common. One of the basics of these religions is Orishas. The people depend on them in every aspect of their lives. When the Afro-Cubans came to the new world, they brought their Orishas with them for support and protection during these tough times. This led to the spread of these beliefs to various places around the world.

Many people found it easy to accept the Orishas. They related to them and their struggles. The people sympathized with the Orishas because they shared similar experiences and were often led by their emotions. Oshun isn't seen as different from any other human. When someone insults her, her ego gets the best of her, and she can be angry and vindictive. She can drown cities to punish sinners. Beautiful and seductive, Oshun is obsessed with her looks. She is aware of her beauty and the impact she has on men. The mirror she carries with her reflects this vanity.

Still, Oshun has a big heart and has often come through to human beings and other Orishas. She is the equivalent of Aphrodite and Venus in Greek and Roman mythology. Her main purpose is to spread love and beauty. She cares for women and their struggles and protects them and their children. There isn't a problem that Oshun can't fix. In most cases, she doesn't resort to violence. She uses her seductive dance moves, beauty, and charm to help her people. It is impossible to deny Oshun's role in mankind. Not only has she assisted with the creation of the universe, but she is the heroine of many legends where she saved the Orishas or mankind using her wit, kind heart, or by sacrificing something. The more you learn about Oshun, the more you will understand why she is significant in these religions and why you need her in your life.

Chapter 2: Are You a Child of Oshun?

Determining who your Orisha is can be a very tricky task. You may feel lost as to where to begin – especially if you're new to the African Traditional faith. In this chapter, you'll learn everything you need to know about mother and father Orishas and head Orishas. You'll find out the difference between them, how to determine who they are, and understand when is the best time to embark on this journey. Finally, you'll understand what it means to be a child of Oshun and find a quiz that will help you determine if you are one.

Mother and Father Orishas

According to the Traditional African faiths, everyone is assigned a biological mother and father and spiritual Orisha mother and father figures upon birth. The Orisha mother ensures your safety, well-being, and protection throughout your life. Your Orisha parents are the ones who guide you, help you when you run into challenges, and look after your happiness. You can only unlock your destiny when you work with your mother and father Orishas, and accept their guidance.

According to African traditions, everyone is assigned spiritual mothers and fathers upon birth.
https://unsplash.com/photos/r6_xcsNg0kw

Each Orisha embodies one of Olodumare's archetypes to serve as an intermediate between worshippers and the Supreme God. There are 4oo+1 Orishas, each of whom rules over a certain aspect of life. This numeric representation shows how limitless the pantheon is. While there isn't an infinite number of Orishas, the "+1" suggests that you can never name all 400, even if you know them all. You will always likely miss at least 1.

There are specific Orishas for everything, from wisdom to healing. Since each person faces the most difficulties in a certain aspect of their life, they are given a personal Orisha at birth – one who is considered to be the person's destined helper. That said, you can still invoke *any Orisha* when you're facing certain troubles in your life. For example, someone who always ends up in toxic romantic relationships should consider working with Oshun. A person who's embarking on a healing journey will need the assistance of Obatala.

If you wish to learn more about your parent Orishas, you must first release any expectations you may have. Your Orishas are seldom who you think they are, so any previous attachments may affect your ability to determine who your parent Orishas are. Also, your Orishas are not necessarily the same as your parents. If your elders follow the African Traditional faith, you should consider talking to them; they are the best teachers you can turn to. Not only do your elders know you since birth, but they are also very wise and experienced and have likely been working with the Orishas for a long time now. They can give you insight and clarity into who your Orisha mother and father are.

If your elders have different spiritual beliefs or it's not possible to contact them directly, you can look at your dreams. Dreams can give you a lot of information and clues into who your Orishas are. Deconstruct the message and, if needed, consult a Babalawo. If all else fails or you're still uncertain, you can ask the Orishas themselves and work with them with the help of a priest or priestess. A specialized Babalawo may even be able to help you out right away based on your answer to certain questions.

Once you determine who your Orisha mother and father are, you need to learn more about them. Read all about their traditions, symbols, preferences, and traditions. Build them an altar and find out which elements and associations to decorate the space with. Find out which offerings they enjoy and make sure you leave gifts for them, and pray to them regularly. Keep the space clean and well-organized, and always approach it with positivity and respect. You should consciously and actively make an effort to connect to your parent Orishas on a deeper level because they're vital figures in your life. Show them that you're committed to working with them so they can offer you the guidance you need.

Head Orisha

Head Orishas are commonly known as tutelary Orishas in African Traditional Religions. Several traditions believe that you can either have two parent Orishas or a single head Orisha or Ori Orisha. Head Orishas act as balancing and guiding entities like mother and father guardians. You don't get to choose your head Orisha, as it is associated with your destiny. This Orisha is the source of spiritual energy a person needs to lead a harmonious life.

You can know who your head Orisha is by undergoing a specialized ceremony. This ritual, however, can only be conducted once in a person's lifetime. Once you know who your head Orisha is, they hold a place in your spirit and soul. You must be aware that you will be committed to your tutelary (custodial) Orisha once you find out who they are. This is why you must be certain you're ready for initiation and this lifelong undertaking. Many practitioners believe that a person becomes a "prisoner" of their chosen faith once the head Orisha settles in. When you dedicate yourself to this spiritual system, you are expected to undergo a series of appropriate initiations, which are often costly. Your head Orisha expects you to be fully brought into the belief system.

If you talk to your elders or other practitioners of the faith, they'll likely tell you to take your time before you learn about your head Orisha, especially if you're still unsure about the spiritual direction you wish to take. If you're interested in the African Traditional Religion but aren't sure whether you're ready to commit, you should consider putting off the tutelary Orisha revelation process. Get to know all the aspects of the religion and learn as much information as you can about the Orishas. Avoid getting too attached to a single one, and make sure that you have a good relationship with the entire pantheon. The Orishas feel jealous when a person favors one over the other or pays them more attention. They may also feel confused about who your tutelary guide is. Only when you're ready to get initiated and undergo Ocha should you consider finding out who your head Orisha is.

You're probably wondering how you can possibly build positive relationships with 401 Orishas. One thing you need to know is that not all Orishas are of equal power and abilities. Only a few of them can seize control of a person's mind. The tutelary Orishas may differ from one faith to another. However, according to the Santería Lukumi religion, the Orishas with this capability are Oshun, Obatala, Elegguá, Shango, Oya, Orunmila, Yemaya, Ochosi, and Ogún. All of these, except for Orunmila (who is initiated through Ifá), become an individual's tutelary spirits through Kariocha.

What Does It Mean to Be a Child of Oshun?

Oshun is the goddess of fertility, love, prosperity, and beauty. It would make sense for the children of Oshun to reflect her qualities and embody her energy. The children of a specific Orisha are expected to paint the lives of other people with the blessings of their deities. You would also be accountable for keeping the spirit of Oshun alive in the minds and hearts of other practitioners.

Quiz: Am I the Child of Oshun?

This quiz is not meant to replace the formal and traditional process of uncovering one's parent or head Orisha. This quiz, however, can help you gain insight into who your Orisha might (or might not) be. It can also allow you to confirm your suspicions and the validity of past evidence that you may be the child of Oshun.

Mark the statements that apply:

1. You enjoy living in luxury and constantly pursue a wealthy lifestyle.
2. You find that wealth and money are very important aspects of life.
3. You enjoy showing off your expensive possessions to others.
4. You wear designer clothes and love to accessorize.
5. You invest in technologies that make your life easier and more comfortable.
6. Some people believe that you're hopeless when it comes to managing your finances.
7. Gold is your favorite color.
8. You like working with gemstones like Carnelian, Agate, Brown Jasper, and Blue Calcite.
9. You care a lot about the opinions of others.
10. You worry about what other people say and think about you.
11. You care a lot about your appearance and reputation.
12. You consider yourself a highly determined individual.
13. You're always driven by your goals and believe you have a greater purpose in life.
14. You plan strategically and never give up on your goals.
15. You are ready to fight for the things you want, even if it means that you need to manipulate others in the process.
16. You enjoy positions that allow you to influence others.
17. You are a natural-born entrepreneur.
18. You don't thrive in commercial or corporate environments.
19. You are a competent and dedicated employee.
20. Your sex life is interesting and intense.
21. Many people claim that you're very flirtatious.
22. You lead by your emotions.
23. You are highly sensitive and responsive to the needs of others.
24. You have a tendency to gain weight.
25. You are very charismatic, loving, and welcoming.

26. If you have children, you're often praised for how you care for them.

27. While you don't like to force your opinions on others, you don't like it when others contradict you.

28. You don't get angry easily, but when you do, it is intense.

29. You are highly affectionate and compassionate.

30. You easily get jealous in romantic relationships, and you have possessive tendencies.

31. Love can make you blind.

32. You like to do everything with your partner, but you realize self-love is more important.

33. You are fair and honest.

Answers Analysis

You are likely a child of Oshun if most of the statements above apply to you.

Oshun is usually depicted as a beautiful woman with charisma, playfulness, and charm. Her clothes are gold and very luxurious, and she's often portrayed wearing expensive jewelry. Oshun enjoys showcasing her breathtaking possessions. Some depictions of Oshun show her holding a mirror, causing her to appear vain. The children of Oshun are expected to have similar expensive tastes, justifying the first 8 statements.

Oshun is known to worry a lot about what other people think and say, which is why her children are also expected to worry about public opinion (statements 9 and 10). She is highly fixated on maintaining a beautiful appearance and an esteemed reputation. She steers clear of scandals and anything that may slightly tarnish her image (statement 11).

Oshun is an archetype of strategic thinking and planning. Her kind and beautiful exterior manipulate and trick others into thinking she doesn't have what it takes to get whatever she wants. Little do they know, however, that she's highly determined and desires social influence and affluence (statements 12 through 19).

Oshun is often portrayed with a honeypot wrapped around her waist. This is a symbol of male sexual pleasure, pregnancy, and fertility. Oshun's children are expected to embody her sensual, seductive, and charming energy (statements 20 and 21).

Oshun is popularly known for being the most sensitive and emotional of all the Orishas in the pantheon. She is even thought to be whiny and reserved at times. Her sensitivity, however, is what makes her attentive to the needs and well-being of others. She is believed to be the protector of the sick and poor and is associated with healing and prosperity. She brings abundance into the lives of others. Even though she's very kind and giving, she can get really angry when someone steps on her toes. She's understanding and tolerant but doesn't like it when someone disagrees with her. Oshun knows when giving becomes too much, as she always prioritizes her well-being. She loves others, but she loves herself more. The children of Oshun are never sheepish when it comes to giving love and showing care, but they know better than to compromise their own needs and welfare. They are affectionate with their partners, friends, and family (statements 22 through 32).

Even though she can get manipulative, if need be, Oshun likes to do things the right way. She is righteous and values qualities like honesty and fairness, especially when dealing with people who deserve this treatment (statement 33).

Now that you know everything you need about mother, father, and head Orishas, you can determine if you're ready to know who they are. You must remember that finding your head Orisha is a lifelong commitment. You must be completely ready to undergo the initiation process.

Chapter 3: Oshun in Myths and Legends

Oshun is among the most prominent figures in Yoruba, Santeria, and Ifa. She plays a role in many stories in African mythology, either as the main character or featured in a supporting role that impacts the story's events.

This chapter will cover myths and legends about Oshun. These will reflect her significance, true character, and relationship with other Orishas.

Oshun has many myths and legends associated with her.
https://www.flickr.com/photos/fenixcsmar/33227614663

Betrayal

One day, the Orishas met to discuss their place in the hierarchy. They were displeased that Olodumare had all the power and that they had to consult him before making any decision. The Orishas were very involved in the affairs of mankind and were doing all the work. Not only was Olodumare a distant deity, but he was also getting old and didn't have any direct influence on people. The Orishas thought that if anyone should be in charge, it should be them.

They decided to rebel against Olodumare. They would no longer follow the deity's orders and would run the universe on their own terms. Eshu (also spelled Esu and Eschu and referred to as Elegba in Santeria) was the Orisha of trickery, similar to Loki from Norse mythology, and was the messenger between the Orishas and mankind. He was a devoted and good friend to Oshun. Eshu was also the Orisha of crossroads. He stood at the doorway, so he heard their rebellious plan.

Eshu ran to Olodumare to tell them about the Orishas' treachery. Olodumare was furious and felt betrayed. The deity had always trusted the Orishas and held them in high regard, which made their actions unjustified and hurtful. Olodumare decided to punish the Orishas by preventing rainfall which then caused a drought. This was the high price paid by the Orishas and mankind alike. The rivers and lakes dried up, plants died, crops failed, humans suffered, and the Earth was perishing. Everything the Orishas created and built was dying. Humans were crying and begging for their help. They thought they had done something to anger the Orishas and asked for forgiveness. However, the Orishas knew that it was all their fault and not the fault of mankind.

The Orishas repented for their actions, cried, and wailed for Olodumare to forgive them. However, Olodumare lived far away in heaven and couldn't hear them. The only solution was for the Orisha to travel to Olodumare and beg for his forgiveness. However, many tried and failed.

Oshun offered to make the journey for the sake of mankind and the universe. However, the Orishas mocked her because she was young and small in size, and she wouldn't be able to succeed, especially when other elder Orishas had failed. They made fun of her vanity and told her to just focus on looking pretty. However, Oshun was much stronger than she looked, and she persisted. The Orishas were desperate and had no other choice. They figured there was no harm in letting her try. However, they all expected her to fail.

She transformed into a peacock and flew away. It was a very long road and close to the sun. Oshun lost her wing feathers and was extremely exhausted, yet she kept flying because she was determined to reach Olodumare. She fell very ill, but nothing could stop her.

Oshun finally made it to Olodumare, but she was so sick she couldn't speak. She fainted in his arms. She was no longer a beautiful peacock but a worn-out vulture. The deity looked after her until she was able to speak. Oshun explained that the Orishas were remorseful and begged for the deity's forgiveness. Olodumare was impressed by Oshun's sacrifice and determination and accepted her apology. The deity explained that her bravery warmed his heart. Olodumare brought back the rain, and all was well again.

Olodumare didn't forget about Oshun's heroic actions. He healed her wings and bestowed on her a huge honor. She became Olodumare's messenger and the only Orisha the deity would communicate with and allow in his realm. Oshun flew back to the Orishas in her vulture form. She had saved the world, and everyone was grateful for her heroism.

Oshun, the River Orisha

Oshun wasn't originally the Orisha of the river. It was Yemaya, the mother of all Orishas and Orisha of the water. Some legends describe her as Oshun's mother, while others say she was her elder sister. All the main Orishas were older than her and had their own realms. Since she didn't have a palace to reside in, Oshun lived a carefree life traveling the world. One day, as she was wandering around, she encountered Ogun. Ogun was a warrior and the Orisha of iron known for his strength and intelligence. When he saw Oshun, he was mesmerized by her beauty.

Ogun wanted Oshun and chased her across the land. She wasn't interested and ran away from him. However, she had nowhere to hide and, as she was running, she fell into the river. The river was dragging her away. When Yemaya saw Oshun, she ran to her rescue. Yemaya realized her daughter needed protection and must have her own realm. Hence, she gave her domain over the rivers and fresh waters.

Oshun and Shango Love Story

One day, Oshun was attending a drumming festival. There was a very handsome man dancing like no one she had ever seen before. Oshun, who had many admirers, felt enamored by him. This man was Shango, the Orisha of lightning and thunder, the equivalent of Thor in Norse mythology. When Shango laid eyes on Oshun, he was taken in by her beauty. No man could ever resist Oshun, and Shango was no different. He was already married to Oba, the Orisha of time and the river Oba. She was also Yemaya's daughter and Oshun's sister.

Shango was a womanizer and desired Oshun, and the feeling was mutual. He and Oshun got married. Although Shango later took a third wife, Oshun remained his favorite. She was a very skilled cook and managed to please Shango with her delicious meals.

Jealousy

Shango was madly in love with Oshun, and he never stopped desiring her, even after they were married. He never got enough of her or her delicious cooking. This broke Oba's heart, who felt that Oshun was taking her place. Oba wanted Shango to desire her in the same way, so she sought her sister's help. She asked her for the secret that made her food irresistible.

Oshun was jealous of Oba and her relationship with Shango. Although Shango truly loved Oshun, Oba had a very special place in his heart which was very hard for her to accept. Oshun decided to cause a rift between them. She told Oba if she wanted Shango to enjoy her cooking and be drawn to her, she should cut off her ear and add it to the food. At first, Oba wasn't convinced and thought her sister may have lied to her. Oshun decided to play a trick on her to make her lie more believable.

Oshun prepared a dish for Shango, added a type of mushroom resembling an ear, and wore a scarf. Shango ate the food and was very pleased. When Oba saw what she thought was the truth, she cut off her ear and used it to prepare a dish for Shango.

Shango ate the meal and enjoyed it. When Oba found her husband loved her food, she decided to tell him the truth so he would know how much she loved him and sacrificed for him. Oba took off her scarf, revealing her missing ear. When Shango found out what she did, he was enraged and disgusted. He couldn't look at Oba's face as she was mutilated. He kicked her out and went to live with Oshun, who was very pleased with herself. Not only did she humiliate Oba, but she also got rid of her.

Oba was heartbroken because she truly loved Shango. She kept weeping and wailing until she turned into the Oba River.

In another version of the myth, Oshun was jealous of Oba because her children would inherit Shango's kingdom one day. When Oba asked for her help, Oshun told her that she had once cut off a piece of her ear and added it to a dish she was making for Shango. Ever since he ate it, she became his favorite wife. Oba couldn't believe that her sister was so gullible to trust her with this secret. She decided to outdo her and cut off her whole ear.

Shango discovered the ear while he was eating. He was furious and felt betrayed because he thought Oba was trying to poison him. His anger was so out of control that he caused thunder to hit his home. Oba and Oshun were terrified and tried to escape, but both women fell and turned into rivers that bore their names.

Oshun's Sacrifice

Yemaya was married to Arganyu, who was one of the eldest Orishas. Some legends say he was Shango's father, while others called him his brother. Yemaya and Arganyu were madly in love. They stayed married for a very long time, and their union benefited mankind. However, Yemaya felt that this relationship had to end. She wanted to spend her life serving the world, but her marriage to Arganyu was holding her back. She wasn't learning anything new and wanted to do more and make a real difference. Yemaya decided to separate from her husband. However, she loved him deeply and didn't want to leave him alone. She wanted Arganyu to be with someone who would take care of him, fulfill his needs, and help him get over her. She knew there was no one better suited for the job than her favorite daughter, Oshun. She wasn't only the Orisha of love but also very beautiful, and no man could resist her. She could also use enchantments and magic on Arganyu so he could forget about Yemaya.

Yemaya headed to her daughter's house to talk to her. Oshun loved her mother so much and was very happy to see her. However, she felt that something was wrong since Yemaya rarely visited anyone, and she also had a concerned look on her face. Oshun fell at Yemaya's feet to show her respect and devotion. She told her that she would do whatever she asked of her. Yemaya held her daughter and was touched by her loyalty. She looked at her face and couldn't help but admire her beauty. She knew that Oshun was the only person who could make Arganyu happy.

Yemaya opened her heart to Oshun and explained her desire. Oshun was shocked as she didn't expect her mother to ask something like that of her. She felt she had spoken too soon by agreeing to the request before knowing what it was. Oshun found herself in a terrible position. She didn't want to go back on her word, but she also couldn't marry a man she didn't love. Yemaya explained her plan to her daughter. She would bring Arganyu here and then make an excuse and leave. Oshun should then start flirting with Arganyu and have sex with him.

After Yemaya left, Oshun pondered what her mother had asked of her. She was still in shock at the request. How could she marry a man she didn't love? There was no denying that Arganyu was good-looking, but she didn't have any feelings for him. However, her mother had told her this was for the greater good, and Oshun loved and respected her mother so much that she couldn't say no.

Oshun couldn't sleep. She knew that her life would never be the same again. She was worried about how Arganyu would react. She loved her mother so much and couldn't get angry or be unkind to her. She decided to accept her mother's request and fell asleep ready to prepare for the big day.

The next morning, Yemaya took Arganyu to Oshun. They didn't speak much on the journey as her mind was preoccupied. She was going to abandon the man she loved forever. Oshun prepared herself and made sure to look her best. Yemaya and Arganyu arrived and saw Oshun; she had never looked more beautiful. After some time, Yemaya excused herself while giving her daughter a look that she should execute the plan. Oshun nodded to reassure her mother. Yemaya embraced her husband, and he knew then that he would never see her again. He felt that his heart was breaking as he saw her walking away.

There was a very long silence before Arganyu began speaking. He wasn't as angry as Oshun had feared. Arganyu was calm and spoke in a soft voice. He told her she didn't need to do that, he would be fine, and she didn't have to displease her mother. Oshun stared at Arganyu without saying a word. She thought about what would happen next and realized that the situation wasn't as horrible as she initially thought. Both agreed to stay together. Arganyu found Oshun beautiful and wanted to keep her word to her mother.

Arganyu was the first man she had ever been with, as this story took place before she met Shango. Although they were never in love, Arganyu was very special to Oshun because he made her feel like a woman. They lived together for a long time in peace and harmony.

Oshun and Ogun

As the Orisha of iron, Ogun worked as a blacksmith. The other Orishas and all of mankind benefited from his work. However, he was tired and wanted to retreat to the forest, where he felt happiest. He knew no one could stop him because he was strong and powerful. One day, he decided to leave and went to live in the forest. However, his absence was noticed. The universe needed a blacksmith to make tools and build things. The Orishas agreed to go to the woods and convince Ogun to come back. None of them were successful. Ogun chased any Orisha who came to visit him out and was adamant about remaining in his new life.

Oshun was the only Orisha who had never tried her luck with Ogun. One day, she went to the other Orishas and asked permission to speak with Ogun. Again, the Orishas underestimated her because of her young age and lack of experience. They were also worried because she was small, and Ogun was very strong and unpredictable. However, Oshun was determined and asked them to give her a chance. She explained that she was stronger than she looked and that she knew exactly how to bring him back. No one took her seriously. They all underestimated her because of her age and naivety.

Obatala, the sky father, creator of mankind, and the father of all Orishas, including Oshun, was present. After a while, he signaled with his hand for everyone to stop talking. Silence filled the room. He said that since all Orishas failed to bring Ogun back, there was no harm in giving Oshun a chance. Obatala knew Oshun was desirable and could entice Ogun and bring him back.

Oshun headed to the forest, ready to execute her plan. She stood in the middle of the forest and started dancing. She wasn't wearing anything but five transparent scarves. Ogun was taking a walk, and when Oshun saw him, she started dancing in a seductive way. She pretended she didn't see Ogun and started singing. He heard her voice and approached to see where it was coming from. Oshun noticed and adjusted the scarves to reveal parts of her body. When she saw Ogun, she approached him slowly and cast a spell by applying honey to his lips.

He was mesmerized by her and fell into a trance. Oshun continued pretending that she didn't see him. She kept moving away from the forest and toward the town and applying honey to his lips to prevent the spell from wearing off and keep him entranced. Suddenly, Ogun regained consciousness to find himself in the city surrounded by all of the Orishas. They were so happy to see him and cheered Oshun for successfully returning him. Ogun decided to stay to make it seem that he returned willingly and that he wasn't fooled. From that day, everyone saw Oshun as a capable and powerful Orisha.

Cheating Death

A beloved king was lying on his deathbed. He was very sick, and Iku, the god of death, was preparing to take his soul. His people were heartbroken and weren't ready to see their king go. They sought the help of an oracle who told them that Oshun could drive Iku away, but they needed to present a great offering. Oshun felt sorry for the people and was impressed by their devotion to their king. She accepted their offering and went to see Iku, who was at the king's house. She firmly told him to leave the king, but he wouldn't accept.

Oshun told him she wouldn't give up until he left. Iku tried to scare her, but Oshun was brave and wouldn't back down. She got closer to him and touched him in a sensual way. He was confused, and before he realized what was happening, Oshun stole his talisman of power. Iku now had no power and was ashamed that Oshun could trick him. She told him he would only get his talisman back if he agreed to leave. Iku left, and the king lived. Oshun was the only Orisha who was able to cheat death.

Seducing a Ghost

Oya, the Orisha of rebirth and death, was Oshun's sister and Shango's third wife. She was jealous that Shango favored Oshun and only paid attention to her. She played a trick to keep her husband near and prevent him from seeing Oshun. Using her power over the dead, Oya summoned ghosts and made them surround the house so Shango couldn't leave. She knew that he couldn't tolerate the dead, so he wouldn't try to challenge them.

Shango was trapped. Days passed, and Oshun started to worry. Shango never stayed that long without seeing her, so she knew something was wrong. She went to see him, and he told her what Oya had done. Oshun went outside and met with the leader of the ghosts. She did everything she could to make him leave. She flirted with him, offered him rum, and seduced him with her beauty. The ghost caved in and walked away. Shango was able to leave and be with Oshun.

It is very clear from all these legends that Oshun was a strong, determined, brave, confident, and clever woman. People would mock and underestimate her, but she defied all odds, believed in herself and proved everyone wrong. She was courageous and always volunteered to help. Selfless and caring, she didn't gain anything from her actions; she just wanted to do well for the sake of mankind and the Orishas.

In many cases, Oshun used her sexuality to resolve issues. It wasn't only one of her powers and a peaceful way to get things done. However, Oshun made it clear that she was more than just a beautiful woman. Her real powers lay in her personality. You cannot help admiring her.

There are many lessons to learn from these stories, but the most significant is believing in yourself even when no one else does. When someone says you can't do something, tell them to watch while you do it. That was Oshun's attitude, and she always showed the other Orishas how capable she was.

Chapter 4: Connecting to the Divine Feminine

The universe is one gigantic being made of endless energy. It constantly creates and is continuously being created at the same time. Its energy is restless, always buzzing and multiplying, but never diminished or destroyed.

The divine feminine is an energy form that is always present.
https://pxhere.com/en/photo/247503

The universe is also governed by its own set of laws. There are twelve laws. One is the law of polarity, and the other is the law of gender. The law of polarity states that everything exists within a binary dynamic.

Basically, this law states that if there is light, there must also be darkness, and if there is warmth, then there is cold, etc. This contrast did not exist by chance; it was by design. This duality creates harmony and balance; without it, everything would devolve into chaos and destruction.

The law of gender is another vital law. It states that every being exists with its counterpart. It is very similar to the law of polarity but does not serve the same purposes. This law also creates balance and harmony between every energetic being.

Now, you may wonder, how are these universal laws related to the divine feminine? Simply put, the divine feminine could not have come into existence if these two laws did not govern the world. This chapter will give you an in-depth understanding of the divine feminine and its role in the Yoruba tradition.

What Is the Divine Feminine?

A divine feminine is an energy form that takes place in almost everything around you. For example, Mother Earth is the divine feminine. The water, moon, and humans have the divine feminine in them. This energy does not exist in one place or in one creature; it exists anywhere and everywhere.

To understand the divine feminine, its qualities must first be understood. How can you distinguish this energy?

1. Creativity

The divine feminine is full of creative energy. It always creates, and its creations are seen as sacred, beautiful, and unique. Think of the Earth and think of all of its creations. Trees that reach the heavens, delicate flowers drawn with intricate details, or lands that are home to millions of living beings. Think of birds that sing, wolves that howl at the moon, roosters that crow at sunrise, creatures that fly between the clouds, and others that live in the ocean's depths. Mother Nature is in a constant state of creation, and its creativity displays its divine feminine energy.

2. Intuition

Intuition is a powerful sensation exercised by both humans and nature. People are inclined to believe that intuition is a tool humans use, but that is far from the truth. Intuition is an energetic force that can exist anywhere and in anything. For instance, the moon is linked to intuition. Various spiritual faiths and cultures believe that the moon strengthens your intuition. It is believed that it elevates your intuitive abilities. This is why the moon is seen as a divine feminine and is often associated with several goddesses in various cultures.

3. Innate Wisdom and Regeneration

Spirituality links the serpent with divine femininity. Several centuries-old cultures used the snake as a symbol of wisdom and transformation. These two qualities are part of the divine feminine archetype. Humans connected to this energy tend to understand themselves through self-reflection. The act of seeking knowledge from within allows people to access their innate wisdom, eventually leading to a transformative cycle. The snake sheds its skin and becomes a new and enhanced version of itself. The divine feminine also knows when it is time to shed their skin and become an advanced version of who they are.

4. The Giver

The divine feminine is a giver by nature. When people tap into this energy, they become givers too. This means a person is generous with time, love, and effort. They are forgiving and empathetic toward themselves and others. This is reflected in nature too. The best way to understand the giving nature of the divine feminine is to compare it with trees. Trees are givers. They provide shade, fruit, and cleaner air, and they are relaxing to look at. They are home to many animals, and their very existence is a gift for every living creature. Like the tree, the divine feminine is naturally giving. However, because the divine feminine is intuitive and wise, it knows when its generosity is being abused, meaning you do not have to be endlessly giving. However, you will find that you are more generous when you are in tune with your divine femininity.

The Divine Feminine and Its Counterpart

To fully comprehend the divine feminine, you need to understand what exists on the other side of it. The laws of polarity and gender state that everything must exist with its counterpart. This means that the divine feminine is one side of the coin. It does not exist on its own. So, what is on the other side of this sacred coin? The divine masculine. The divine feminine and masculine exist in harmony. Together, these two energies create a necessary equilibrium. Too much of anything can and will create chaos. This is why the divine feminine exists alongside the divine masculine.

This is not to say that one is incomplete without the other. On the contrary, both of these energies are perfect the way they are. However, they each add qualities that the other lacks. For instance, the law of polarity says that everything and its opposite co-exist together, right? So, for instance, the divine feminine is more reflective and seeks wisdom from within. On the other hand, the divine masculine seeks wisdom from the outside or through others.

Of course, this does not mean that one way is better than the other. However, it would not be wise to only seek wisdom from within and to just depend on the outside for insight. This is why it is best to rely on either strategy occasionally.

Now, you must remember that the divine feminine and masculine are energy forces. What does this mean? Simply put, both energies are frequencies anyone can tap into. For instance, it is natural to assume that women are naturally connected to the divine feminine and men tap into the divine masculine, right? Not exactly.

To understand this, you need to look deeper into the components of a human. People physically exist in an earthly plane and spiritually exist in a spiritual realm. The way people understand gender on Earth only works for the physical realm. However, gender does not work the same way in the spiritual world. Why is that? Because spirituality states that gender in the spiritual form is nothing more than energy. What is energy in the spiritual world? In its simplest form, it is a frequency. This means anyone can naturally tap into a certain frequency or consciously switch from one energy to another.

In clearer words, both women and men can tap into either energy. Women can be connected to their divine masculine, and men can act from their divine feminine energy. Humans can also switch between these two energies at any time they want.

Now that you have a good grasp on the divine feminine qualities, it is time to familiarize yourself with the divine masculine so that you can understand the workings of the divine feminine.

The divine masculine is a chaser, meaning it is active and assertive. It is not known for deep self-reflection because it is more focused on setting goals and following through with plans. This energy is more decisive and logical. This does not mean that people who are in tune with their divine masculine are emotionless. On the contrary, they feel their emotions, but they act on their logical side. The divine masculine is naturally protective and has a good sense of leadership.

One can find a good balance between both energies – meaning you can be more in tune with your divine feminine and connected to your divine masculine a second later. You can easily do this when you have good discernment between both and know how you feel when connected to either of them.

The Oshun Archetype and the Divine Feminine

The divine feminine concept is universal. This means various cultures with different backgrounds recognize these sacred energies. Of course, the term "divine feminine" is more westernized. The Yoruba people believe in the divine feminine energy, and they know it as Oshun. Who is Oshun?

Oshun is a Nigerian goddess. She rules the rivers, water, love, sensuality, fertility, and purity. She is portrayed as a gentle and kind goddess, but she is also known for her fiercely protective nature. She is known to take her vengeance on anyone who dares cross her.

The goddess is named after the Osun River in Nigeria. The goddess of the Oceans, Yemaya, and Olofin, king of the skies, were in a union and gave birth to Oshun. The goddess is more in tune with her divine femininity, but she also displays minor divine masculine qualities. This makes her perfectly balanced.

How does the goddess balance both energies? To answer this question, you must first familiarize yourself with Oshun.

Oshun was the only female sent to Earth, along with 16 other male gods. These divine beings were sent to Earth to populate it and create life. The gods attempted to create life, but they failed. Oshun was the only goddess who successfully created life.

Does this remind you of the divine feminine qualities? Oshun used her creativity, inner wisdom, intuition, and fertility to create life. Oshun brought water to the earth, creating and giving life to everything around her. The goddess's impact on Earth was so strong that the Yoruba people believed that humanity would not have existed had Oshun not helped in any way.

The Yoruba people pray to the goddess to help them with their fertility. This shows the goddesses' generosity and love for her devotees. Oshun uses her powers and helps her worshippers by allowing them to create like her. The goddess is pleased when she sees her devotees create and endlessly give and love their creations.

She is a clear example of the divine feminine, but she also connects to her divine masculine when needed. For instance, she protects her creations and children. She is also known to show her wrath when angered. For instance, one myth describes violent floods and heavy rains that destroyed the people who wronged the goddess. These stories display how the goddess is naturally in tune with her divine femininity. Still, she also has the power to connect to her divine masculinity when needed.

Divine Feminine Lore and Proverbs

The Yoruba tradition has several stories of Oshun which display her divine femininity. For instance, one myth describes Oshun as a clever goddess who could cheat death. It was known that certain gods and goddesses could not reach the heavens by themselves. However, Oshun wanted to challenge the Orishas and reach the heavens. The Orishas laughed at the goddess and did not believe she could reach the skies.

Oshun was adamant about reaching the heavens, so she turned herself into a beautiful peacock with colorful feathers. She successfully flew to the sky, but the sun began to burn her feathers away. The sun started eating at her skin, but the goddess continued flying higher. Oshun finally reached the creator, Olodumare. She collapsed in his arms and turned into a vulture. The creator admired her dedication and bravery and nursed the goddess back to health. Olodumare honored Oshun's dedication by only communicating through her.

Since then, the peacock and the vulture became symbols of Oshun's transformation, regeneration, courage, and dedication.

Another myth displays Oshun's intelligence and sensuality. The story begins with Oya, Oshun's sister, and Shango's third wife. Oya was jealous because Shango favored Oshun over her. One day, she summoned a ghost and demanded that it surround the house. Oya knew that Shango did not dare challenge the undead. The ghost haunted their house, per Oya's request, and Shango could not escape the house.

Meanwhile, Oshun was worried because she knew that nothing could keep her husband away from her. She visited the house and found the ghost that Oya had summoned. Oshun tried to make the ghost leave by offering it rum, but the ghost did not leave the house. The goddess then used her sensuality to seduce the ghost into leaving the house. The ghost eventually got scared of Oshun's attempts and left. Once the ghost left the house, Oshun and Shango were reunited.

What do these stories display? They showcase Oshun's divine femininity. As a human, you do not have to use your divine femininity similarly. Through these stories, Oshun shows how anyone can manipulate their divine femininity and use it as a powerful tool to achieve anything their heart desires.

How Can You Connect to the Divine Feminine?

If you want to be in tune with your divine feminine, you must familiarize yourself with its qualities. Now that you know what qualities you must work on, you need to have self-reflection sessions with yourself.

Ask yourself, "What is my relationship with my intuition? Do I listen to my intuition? Do I follow my inner wisdom? Or do I discredit it?" Your relationship with your intuition here is key to connecting with the divine feminine.

Get used to having self-reflection sessions with yourself; if it feels foreign to you, then this is a sign that you must practice self-reflection. That will help you be more in tune with your body and spirit. The more you do this, the more your intuition will be in a smooth flow state.

Remember that the divine feminine is known for its creativity. This does not mean that you need to give birth physically. It simply means that you need to allow yourself to be in a creative flow. Once you allow your creativity to flow through your body, allow yourself to create. Your creations can take on any form: pottery, a piece of fiction, an artistic piece, etc.

The divine feminine is also a giver. Now, ask yourself how I can be more giving. Your generosity should begin with yourself first. This means you must be generous, gracious, and forgiving of yourself first. The more you practice being generous with yourself, the more you will find yourself naturally generous with others.

This may sound daunting at first. Do not worry; there are rituals that you can try to help you connect with your divine femininity.

Self-Love Ritual

Ingredients:

- 1 large white candle
- 5 sunflowers
- 1 teaspoon of cinnamon
- 1 teaspoon of honey
- 1 bowl
- Your signature perfume
- An Oshun statue

Instructions:

1. In a safe space, light a candle for five days in front of the Oshun statue.
2. Place the candle in the center of the bowl.
3. Dress the bowl and candle with cinnamon, honey, and sunflowers.
4. Converse with Oshun during the five days and ask her to help you find your sensuality or to help you fall in love with yourself.
5. On the fifth day, blow out the candle.
6. Remove the candle and any leftover wax. Take the bowl with its ingredients and fill it with warm water.
7. Step into the shower.
8. As you pour the water, pray to the goddess.

Fertility Ritual

Ingredients:

- 1 large yellow candle
- 1 teaspoon of honey
- 1 pumpkin
- 1 pencil
- An Oshun statue

- 1 brown paper bag

Instructions:

1. Light the candle.
2. Leave it in a safe space.
3. Light it for five days.
4. Pray to the goddess and share your wishes with her.
5. Create a large opening on top of the pumpkin.
6. Cut out a piece of paper from the brown paper bag.
7. Use your pencil and write your wishes on it.
8. Place the paper in the pumpkin.
9. Seal the pumpkin with candle wax.
10. Place the sealed pumpkin on top of your stomach so that you can conceive.
11. Place the pumpkin and leave it next to a river as an offering for the goddess.

To summarize, the divine feminine is an energetic force. It is a state of mind that anyone can tap into. You do not need to be a man or a woman to be connected with their divine femininity. Remember that you can shift between the divine feminine and masculine whenever you want to. Most importantly, remember that balance is key between both energies. You can be naturally more in tune with your divine femininity, but remember to connect with your divine masculine as well. Whenever you need to connect with the sacred feminine energy, pray to Oshun or read stories about her and let her inspire your divine feminine.

Chapter 5: Plants, Symbols, and Offerings

Now that you know how to connect to the divine feminine, you're ready to learn what offerings to place on your altar or in any other of her favorite places. By reading this chapter, you'll uncover what the goddess of love and prosperity prefers to receive as offerings and what symbols or objects you can use to invoke her powers. It lists Oshun's associated plants, animals, symbols, flowers, fruit, meals, and so on - including the reasons they relate to the goddess. You'll also find a few recipes for meal offerings you can prepare on any day you wish to honor Oshun.

Plants Associated with Oshun

Like all other Orishas, Oshun also has her representation in herbs and healing plants containing her energy. By using them in spells and rituals devoted to the goddess, you can obtain her ashe and use it to empower yourself in love and other endeavors and acquire success. Below are the most common plants associated with Oshun.

Different herbs and plants are associated with Oshun.
https://unsplash.com/photos/6LTAljmu2cY

Cinnamon

The cinnamon bush is a plant highly associated with Oshun, mainly because it goes well with the sweet recipes the goddess of love prefers. It particularly pairs well with honey, another one of Oshuns natural symbols. Followers of Oshun believe that cinnamon attracts love and good fortune. Apart from offerings, they often use this herb in cleansing rituals before performing a spell or rite for the goddess.

Cinnamon also has medicinal properties and is known to aid digestion, regulate blood sugar levels and boost immunity. Healers often use it in syrups to treat colds and respiratory infections. One of the best ways to honor Oshun is by taking care of your health - and this herb is one of the best tools for that. Being in better shape helps you take better advantage of the blessings the goddess provides.

Cloves

Cloves appeal to Oshun for several reasons. They're associated with protection and empower the practitioner during their work. They also help cleanse the spirit from negative influences, creating space for the goddess's ashe. Cloves embody fertility and can help connect with the goddess when asking for her assistance to make any aspect of life more fertile.

Calendula

Also known as tufted marigold, calendula is a plant infused with incredibly potent energy emanating from the goddess. It has purifying properties, which come in handy for cleansing rituals and prayers you can use to invoke and honor Oshun. It's said to cleanse one's energy and dispel negative influences. All of this is essential for communicating with the goddess.

Calendula infusion treats ear and gum infections, relieves toothache and skin irritations, and regulates the menstrual cycle. Due to the latter effect, the plant contributes to fertility - the primary reason it's linked to Oshun.

Sunflower

The sacred plant of Oshun, the sunflower, has many uses in a wide range of Orisha-related rituals. Its healing properties include relieving symptoms of respiratory infections, fever, colds, nosebleeds, and gastrointestinal conditions. This plant is also effective against kidney infections, kidney stones, and infections of the lower urogenital tract. Because of the latter effect, it has a positive impact on fertility. It enables women who want to conceive to take advantage of Oshun's blessings.

The sunflower is the sacred plant of Oshun.
https://unsplash.com/photos/oO62CP-g1EA

The sunflower is also the symbol of good luck and the beneficial effect of water on nature. Due to Oshun's association with the waters, it's easy to see why she prefers this plant to be given as an offering. Besides water, the sunflower is also known to constantly look for sunlight, attracting good energy to its flowers. You can use it to attract positive energy and empower any spell or ritual you perform in the goddess's name.

Pumpkin

According to the Yoruba lore, Oshun carved the first lamp out of a pumpkin and used it to dance beside. It's also believed that the goddess keeps her riches in pumpkins. These gifts can be accessed with the invisible spells she stores in the rivers, so pumpkins are typically offered to her near running water.

In some traditions, pumpkins cannot be consumed or sold for eating, while other practices use them for their healing properties. It treats digestive issues, burns, and skin inflammation. It can also be used in purification and beauty rituals associated with Oshun. It makes the skin, hair, and nails look healthier, specifically when used with Oshun's blessing. Other uses for pumpkin include spells promoting fertility, brightening one's life, reigniting old relationships, personal growth, success, and more.

Melon

Traditionally, Castille melon is used for this purpose (it's the sweetest one, and Oshun likes things sweet), but any kind of melon will do. Similarly to the pumpkin, melon is offered at the riverbanks or near large bodies of water as this is the best place to reach out to the goddess. If you don't have rivers near you, you can prepare the melon for a spell, ritual, or as a meal offering and serve it at your altar along with saying a prayer to the goddess. Melon is often offered alongside honey and cinnamon, which enhance its powers. The plant has similar properties as pumpkins and is often associated with fertility. It's used in rituals invoking the goddess to make any area of life more fertile.

Yams

Yams have been a staple food in African cultures for centuries. Besides the great flavor that allows them to be incorporated into a variety of meals, yams are also highly fruitful plants. Because of this, they're often associated with fertility. Yams are often used in offerings for this cause or simply because the goddess favors them. They are typically offered alongside honey or incorporated into a honey-sweetened meal.

Oranges

Oranges are also sweet fruits Oshun loves to receive in offerings. Orange seeds appeal to her even more as they're associated with fertility and new life. Place the seeds on your altar in a small bowl of honey after removing them from an orange you've eaten. Say a prayer to the goddess, and she will grant your wishes regarding fertility. Oranges are also packed with vitamins you can use to boost your immunity and prepare yourself for the blessing you're about to receive.

River Flax

If you live near a river, you'll come across river flax, a type of grass favored by Oshun in rituals and offerings. One of the common ways river flax is used to obtain the goddess's favor is a five-day ritual performed at a riverbank. On the first day, a stone symbolizing Oshun is put in honey, after which she is offered her favorite animals (nowadays only symbolically). On the second day, the honey is removed from the stone, and the stone is covered with a yellow linen sheet. On the third day, the person performing the ritual fans themselves five times (traditionally with five different fans, but you can use one). On the fourth day, Oshun is offered five different natural sweets. Until this time, everything is done at an altar. On the fifth day, the stone is carried to the river and placed in a basket together with a piece of gold. The basket is traditionally sent toward the middle of the water for the river to carry it away. You can also leave it at the riverbank while dedicating a prayer to the goddess, asking her for her blessings.

Hawksbill

According to Yoruba beliefs, Oshun requires the hawksbill plant when she is asked for a more extensive favor. It's her way of ensuring the requester is empowered through the plant and is ready to receive the goddess's ashe. It's typically used as a seat (put under) for shells containing spiritual water. At other times, the plant is infused to create the spiritual herbal water needed for spells, rituals, and offerings.

Freshness

This unique herb grows in humid soil, such as that found near rivers and other bodies of water - hence why the goddess prefers it. It's believed that it attracts good fortune and wards off evil spirits. It's often used for the cleansing rituals enacted for homes and to help the soul prepare for the goddess's blessings. It can also be infused into water, which is used to clean the floors. Another way to use freshness-infused water is to drink it. It improves kidney function, which further purifies the body from negative influences. You can leave it on your altar for a day and ask the goddess to bless it, then drink it or use it for its intended purpose.

Macaw

In South America, Oshun is often offered yellow macaw. The roots, leaves, and stems have medicinal properties. These can treat digestive issues, regulate the metabolism, and relieve chronic pain. However, Oshun prefers the flowers of this plant in offerings because they help cleanse the spirit from harmful energies. You can ask the goddess to bless the flowers on your altar and use them in a cleansing bath. This way, you'll be ready for Oshun's blessings.

Parsley

Parsley is commonly used in food. It is also another one of Oshun's favorites. It has many uses in folk medicine due to its antioxidant, immune-boosting, anti-inflammatory, and cleansing properties. You can offer parsley as part of any meal offerings you prepare for Oshun, in teas, or as a part of a cleansing ritual. Depending on how you use it, parsley can purity the body, mind, and spirit. All this is essential for receiving blessings - whether you ask for fidelity, love, or prosperity.

Oshun's Animals and Other Symbols

Besides plants, Oshun is also associated with several animals and other symbols.

Sacred Birds

Oshun's sacred animals are clever birds, such as vultures and peacocks. According to Yoruba lore, when some of the Orishas rebelled against the supreme rule of Olodumare, Oshun summoned her sacred birds for protection against the creator's wrath. Her sacred birds helped protect Oshun and the rest of the Orishas, for which she will always cherish them and prefer their symbolism in offerings. These sacred birds symbolize Oshun's courage and ability to stand up for herself and others and persevere. Because they prefer to live near water, these birds are associated with the goddess. For the same reason, they're also linked to healing and life. It's believed the Oshun sacred birds can carry on their healing powers through the water and grant assistance in fertility, cleansing, and love spells and rituals. You can use symbols or images of these birds or feathers if you can obtain them. Place these on your altar when invoking the goddess for a protection spell or ritual.

The peacock is one of the sacred birds due to their intelligence.
https://unsplash.com/photos/_7S3tOs424o

Honey

Oshun is often portrayed with a honeypot at her waist. According to ancient beliefs, honey symbolizes fertility and sexual pleasure, which, in turn, is often linked to pregnancy. It's said that women who want to conceive should offer honey to Oshun, asking her to bless them with a child. As another form of honoring Oshun as the fertility goddess and depicting her powers of femininity and sensuality, women often carry honey cakes with them or wear honey (or golden) colored beads and belts around their waist.

Another way to use honey when asking for Oshun's blessings is in spells and rituals. Like all sweet things associated with the goddess, honey can also help you attract good luck, wealth, and prosperity. You can incorporate this into any work you perform for this purpose, ask the goddess for assistance, and you'll receive what you desire in abundance. Oshun will particularly appreciate it if you taste the honey before incorporating it into your work.

Essential Oils

Oshun prefers essential oils extracted from her favorite plants, herbs, and spices. However, you can use your favorite oils, even if they aren't on her preferred list. The goddess is guaranteed to like them as long as they're colorful, fragrant, and have an air of sensuality. The best way to incorporate essential oils into spells, rituals, and offerings made for Oshun is to pair them with cinnamon, cloves, and other dry spices she likes.

Running Waters

As the goddess of rivers, Oshun prefers her offerings to be left near running water, such as rivers and waterfalls. If you don't have a running or sweet water source nearby, you can use their symbols at your altar. For example, you can use the picture of a waterfall when you ask for purification, healing, or warding off hostile influences. If you have these sources nearby but can't (or prefer not to) leave offerings out in nature, you can take some from the source of that water. Bring it home and place it on your altar next to the other offerings you've prepared for the goddess.

Items of Value

While Oshun is traditionally associated with the color gold and gold items, other items of value also appeal to her. When followers ask for significant favors, including fertility and financial prosperity, they typically offer gold coins or objects. Brass and copper are also great alternatives to gold items.

Incense

Due to its light sweet aroma, Oshun particularly loves sandalwood incense. It's associated with protection and will help you evoke the goddess's protective powers. However, once again, you can use any sweet incense you prefer during your work. Oshun can infuse her powers into anything sweet; incense makes this even easier as it permeates your senses. It envelops your body and spirit and wards off any negative energies which threaten to disrupt your work.

Cowrie Shells

According to ancient lore, Obatala passed on his divinatory powers to Oshun with the help of cowrie shells. When Obatala needed to retrieve his belongings from Elegba, he asked Oshun to do it for her and, in turn, taught her how to use the shells for divination. As she was about to complete her task, she was instructed by Elegeba to train the other Orishas to divine using cowrie shells. The Orishas, in turn, taught the humans this art. These shells then became associated with prophecy and Oshun. They're used in rituals, spells, and offerings made in her honor.

Cowrie shells can evoke her and ask her for guidance regarding success or spiritual growth. Cowrie shells also symbolize waters and water creatures Oshun rules over. Anytime you need cleansing or to evoke the power of water and its creatures, you can incorporate cowrie shells (or any other shells you can find) into your work with the goddess.

Drinks

Oshun loves sweet drinks, typically made from fruit. Orange juice is one of her favorites, but chamomile tea appeals to her also, especially if it's sweetened with honey. The goddess also likes sweet white wines as an offering - particularly if they are accompanied by one of her favorite meals.

Femininity Symbols

Oshun is one of the most empowering female deities, but even she loves to be reminded of her femininity. Using femininity symbols is also great for female followers as it helps them embrace their feminine side without having to compromise other aspects of life. You can offer the goddess makeup, perfume, brushes, and other products associated with feminine beauty - even if you don't use them yourself every day. Alternatively, you can recite a prayer to the goddess after a cleansing and pampering ritual or while looking at your own image in the mirror. The latter is an incredibly empowering experience for those looking to enhance some parts of themselves to attract love.

Recipes for Honoring Oshun

While she loves fruit and drinks more, Oshun won't turn her back on some of the following meal offerings either.

Oshun's Butternut Squash Soup

This soup can be offered alongside spells and small rituals for love or prosperity. As the goddess who is always willing to embrace her feminine powers, Oshun is ready to show her talents in the kitchen too. According to lore, her favorite foods were pumpkins and melons. Therefore, this butternut squash recipe is one of the best ways to honor her in your meal offerings. Serve on the altar or a table covered with gold or yellow cloth to represent Oshun's traditional colors. The recipe is enough for at least four people, so feel free to share it with your friends or loved ones.

Ingredients:

- 2 cups of chicken broth
- 3 cups of butternut of cleaned squash cubes
- 2 tablespoons of butter
- Half an onion
- 1/4 cup of applesauce
- ½ teaspoon of dried parsley
- ¼ teaspoon of ground sage plus more for garnish
- ½ teaspoon of onion powder (optional for added flavor)
- Pinch of ground nutmeg
- Pinch of ground cinnamon
- ¼ cup of cooking cream
- Sunflower or dried pumpkin seeds (optional for garnish)

Instructions:

1. In a large saucepan, melt the butter on low heat. While it melts, mince the onion.
2. Transfer the onion to the pan and cook until it becomes translucent.
3. In another pan, add the squash and cover it with water. Bring to a boil and simmer until it becomes tender when pierced with a fork.
4. When the squash is cooked, drain it, mash it, and transfer it into the pan with the onion.
5. Add applesauce, spices, and chicken broth, and mix until well combined.
6. Bring to a boil again, and cook for 10 minutes on low heat while stirring frequently.
7. Remove from the heat, and add salt, pepper, and cream. Serve with sage and, eventually, sunflower or pumpkin seeds for a garnish.

Oshun's Honey Yams

This recipe is perfect for celebrating the goddess on her feast day. However, you can also prepare it whenever you need empowerment from her or want to celebrate your connection. She is extremely fond of yams and honey - and this recipe is another of her favorites. She'll grant your wishes if you seek her help with fertility, wealth, or anything else she has power over. The recipe only has a few ingredients and takes no time at all to prepare, so you'll have plenty of time to prepare other meals and offerings to celebrate the goddess. You can place a plate of yams for her on your altar or a table covered with golden or yellow cloth and eat one yourself while celebrating Oshun.

Ingredients:

- 2 - 3 yams (if you're eating alongside Oshun, you'll need 3)
- 2 teaspoons of dried chamomile flowers
- 3 tablespoons of raw honey
- 2 cinnamon sticks

Instructions:

1. Pour water into a medium pot and bring it to a boil.

2. Break the cinnamon sticks in half and add them to the water along with the dried chamomile.

3. Add the yams to the pot, and bring them to a boil once again. Cook until the yams become tender.

4. Once the yams become as soft as you prefer them, remove the pot from the heat, drain the water, and peel the yams. (You can peel them before boiling, but it's easier to remove their skin when they're cooked).

5. Mash the yams or cut them into bite-sized pieces depending on your preferences. Add a little ground cinnamon and honey on top, and the goddess won't be able to resist it - and neither will you.

Chapter 6: Creating an Altar for the Goddess

Although not all devotees see creating an altar as a compulsory part of their practice, those who do agree that having a dedicated spiritual center for any purpose has many advantages. Regarding Oshun, having a place where you can connect with her through daily rituals is particularly beneficial for your health and spiritual growth. Reading this chapter, you will learn about the additional benefits of creating an altar for Oshun in or near your home and using this space to celebrate the goddess and the divine feminine within you. You will be provided with plenty of user-friendly tips for fashioning a shrine to Oshun, learning how to care for it, and how to use it to make offerings to this Orisha. That said, the advice from this chapter should only serve as a starting point. Some elements in a shrine are necessary to venerate the goddess of love and prosperity. That said, feel free to add personal touches to your creation to empower your sacred spiritual space completely. Not only will this enable you to form an unbreakable bond with Oshun, but it will allow you to strengthen yourself spiritually.

Make sure your altar represents aspects to help you celebrate Oshun.
https://www.rawpixel.com/image/5943767/free-public-domain-cc0-photo

The Benefits of Creating an Altar for Oshun

A sacred place for one's spiritual practice is vital to many belief systems, including the Yoruba, Ifa, and Santeria. Many followers of these religions believe that having a holy place dedicated to your practice has benefits for your spirit and your connection with your guides and the Orishas you worship. Below are a few of the greatest gifts you can attain by creating an altar for the goddess Oshun.

Gaining a Space for Invoking the Goddess

Oshun's favorite places to hang around? Rivers! However, if you don't have those nearby, the next best place to invite her is a sacred space dedicated to her. Each item you place on the altar connects to your soul and the spirit of the goddess you want to evoke. The items you use to decorate your Oshun altar represent emotions and intentions. They also denote symbols that can help you grow spirituality, find love (including self-love), achieve prosperity, and more. You will have a straightforward way to communicate with Oshun through the shrine you've erected and maintained in her honor. The more you use this place to call on her, the more power (ashe) you can harness throughout your spiritual practice. From the elements representing Oshun to your offerings for her, the items you place on the goddess's altar will help you become more confident in your goals - just as Oshun was always in hers.

Whether you're a child of Oshun or a simple devotee, building a relationship with her involves using a dedicated space for several days. Not only that, but you'll be required to place new symbols on the altar each day. Whether you exchange the existing ones or add new items depends on the objective of your spiritual work. Either way, using an altar will empower you spiritually and deepen your connection to this Orisha. You can also share the space with others who want to connect to the divine feminine. It's a wonderful way for devotees to find common ground and empower each other's sensuality and self-confidence through mutual practice.

Focusing on Your Intentions

Whether you communicate with Oshun daily or only during the days associated with her and festivals, having a space dedicated to this can help you focus on your intention every time. As you decorate the altar, you will already start focusing on your purpose of reaching out to the goddess. As you place her correspondences in front of you, you leave ordinary thoughts and worries behind. Your mind is slowly shifting into a calmer plane, where there is only you, your intention, Oshun, and the tools which help you form a connection with her. For example, if you wake up feeling negative energies lurking around you, your intention could be to ask the goddess to help you dispel them. You can ponder on this while you set up the altar. By the time you've finished and have invited her, she will know how to help you.

Garnering Positive Vibes

There is no better way to celebrate Oshun than to empower yourself with positive energy. Feeling positive gives you confidence and allows you to cultivate self-love - both of which will please the goddess. After all, she is a woman who knows her value and expects her devotees to have the same approach to life. An altar can also be a valuable tool for inviting and retaining her loving energy into your home for an extended period. This is especially helpful if you've been struggling with a lack of confidence and positive thoughts lately. Setting up an altar for the love goddess and caring for it will ensure positive energy continues flowing through your space.

Negative experiences and influences can hinder your ability to grow spiritually, be productive and cultivate self-love. If you've felt their effects, building a shrine to Oshun is the first step toward breaking away from negativity. By making an altar for Oshun, you'll have a space for addressing and counteracting negative influences, regardless of their origins. Whether it comes from malicious spirits or envious living, having a space dedicated to the love goddess will empower you to dispel the negativity from your life and replace it with positive influences.

Learning Oshun's Correspondence

While this book enlists Oshun's correspondences, you, as a novice, aren't expected to learn all of them right away. Building an altar to this goddess can be a wonderful learning experience. During this, you can learn to understand what you should display and why. After visiting this sacred space regularly, you'll know instinctively which color to use and what offerings she prefers. Learning the correspondences of Oshun will let you see firsthand how they work best. This will also help you understand what she dislikes and what to avoid when making offerings for her.

Discovering Your Creative Side

Decorating an altar is an excellent way to express your creativity - even if you didn't think you had one. While there are certain objects you'll need to use, figuring out how to place them requires some creative thought. You'll be surprised to discover how resourceful you can be during this process. It allows you to create something unique and express your thoughts and emotions through your handy work. Whether you revere Oshun as an Orisha, the archetype of the divine feminine, the patron of sweet water, or any of her other aspects, you will always have several options for celebrating her and communicating with her. Whichever your goal is for calling on her, there is a way to express it creatively through the adornments you use for the altar.

Creating a Space for Yourself

By bringing together the right combination of elements, you can create a space to pamper yourself whenever you feel the need to do this. Whether you do this through a spell, ritual, prayer, meditation, or any other means, you can use the altar to invoke Oshun's spirit. As her divine essence permeates your senses, your body and mind relax, and your spiritual experience becomes deeper. After this, you can make an inquiry - using incense and other tools that help you focus on the specific intention you have in mind. Choose the ones that feel right to use in the current situation. Another option is to empower yourself by grounding your mind and body by meditating in front of the offerings dedicated to Oshun. The goddess will show you how to use nature's power to nourish your self-confidence and love so you can achieve your goals. Or, you can pray to Oshun and do other self-empowering exercises, such as saying positive affirmations or praising yourself while looking at yourself in the mirror. Anything you do to elevate your spirit will appeal to the goddess, as she is known to do that for herself too.

Connecting with Nature

Anytime you work with an Orisha, you're getting closer to nature, and forming a connection to Oshun is no exception. This goddess favors natural elements such as herbs, bird feathers, water, and delicious fruit and vegetables. Whether you can grow and harvest these yourself is irrelevant. As long as you express your gratitude for them when placing them on your altar, the goddess will know you respect them just as much as she does. Some of these can be perfect for offerings. In contrast, others can be used in spells and rituals to encourage Oshun to help you gain insight or do any other work which aligns with your traditions and culture. You will leave most of Oshun's correspondences and offerings on the altar for several days (or at least half a day). This is plenty of time for her to notice their presence. Once she does, she will bestow many blessings in return.

How to Build an Altar for the Goddess

From where you place it to the items you put on it, many details go into creating an altar. Here are a few tips for making a shrine for Oshun in or near your home.

Altar Placement

Before you start adorning the altar, you must choose a fitting place for it, ideally in a quiet space in your home. If you live near a river or another freshwater source, you can also set it up near the house and as close to the water as possible. As a general rule of thumb, the altar should always be placed away from high-traffic areas. Otherwise, you won't be able to calm your mind and body, rendering you unable to focus on your intention during your work. It's also a good idea to place the altar in a south-facing room, so you can have as much sunlight as possible. Sunlight is essential for working with Oshun, as it's associated with one of her favorite flowers, the sunflower, which uses sunlight to attract positive energy. Having a sacred place in your bedroom would facilitate morning and evening prayers to the goddess, which are recommended for building a strong bond with her.

If you don't have space for a full table to serve as an altar, you can always set up a smaller area on your dresser, vanity table, or inside your closet. Alternatively, you can set up a small altar on the windowsill. This way, you can leave the window open and bask in the sunlight (unless it's too hot outside) during your work. If you plan to practice meditation or similar self-empowering exercises, set up the altar in a space that can accommodate these activities.

What to Put on the Altar

Creating an altar requires using all the items associated with this goddess:

- A yellow piece of cloth, or several of them, depending on how big your altar is
- Yellow and orange crystals - use real stones, if possible
- Cowrie shells, or, if you can't find these, you can use any variety of shells, or symbols of water creatures
- A small statue or picture of Oshun
- A white plate
- A glass of water (river water works best, but you can also use tap water)
- A glass of white wine (or a bottle if you plan to toast her and drink in her honor)
- A small dish with honey
- Gold coins or jewelry
- 5 pieces of fruit (or whole fruit if you're using smaller yellow or orange fruit)
- Beauty products such as perfume, makeup, and a mirror
- Sunflowers (preferably fresh, but you can also use dry or artificial if they aren't in season)
- Feathers
- 2 Yellow candles
- Sweet incense (or one you prefer)

- A cup of chamomile tea with cinnamon (or just a cinnamon stick)
- Yellow clothes (optional)
- Prepared meals you plan to offer (or raw yams, pumpkins, or other produce she favors)

Healing herbs After gathering your tools and ingredients, you can start setting up the altar:

1. Begin by draping the yellow cloth over the surface of the altar.
2. Place the representation of Oshun in the center and the white plate in front of it. Fill the latter with the offerings.
3. Put one of the candles on the left side of the symbol and the other one on the right-hand side.
4. Place the cup of water next to the left candle, the cup of wine next to the right-hand candle, and the dish with the honey somewhere between the two candles (behind the goddess symbol).
5. After placing the fruit where you have larger bits of space, scatter all the small items that symbolize Oshun.
6. Scatter the sunflowers and the healing herbs between the other items.
7. Take the clothes and leave them on the far left side of the altar.
8. Place the incense on the left. Light it just before you start your work, along with the candles.

How to Make Offerings and Clear Them

Before using the shrine, don't forget to bless the shrine by dedicating a short prayer to the goddess before using it. It's also a good idea to cleanse your space and yourself with smudging and even by taking a cleansing bath before you start working. The latter will put you in a better mood, facilitating your communication with the goddess. Alternatively, you can ground yourself and cleanse yourself through nature's power.

After this, you can start presenting the offerings. If you're working with the goddess daily, be generous, and leave a small item every day. Say a prayer or do a quick meditation every time you do. Don't leave out food items for more than two or three days. If the food is cooked, remove it within eight hours. The sunflowers will also wilt, so you'll need to replace them. Non-perishable items can remain for as long as you need them or until you decide to replace them with other ones.

Apart from the tools listed above, you can also adorn your altar with items that reflect your current needs and wants. The number of smaller objects should be five, the goddess's sacred number. If you think that your altar is getting too crowded, feel free to remove some items. As you continue your daily communication with the goddess, you will soon start adding new ones.

Besides daily veneration and honoring her on her holy days, you can also leave offerings to Oshun when you wish to connect to the divine feminine, re-discover your sensuality, or need a helping hand to find love or the key to prosperity in any area of life.

How to Care for the Altar

For new devotees, having only a small altar in your home is generally recommended - so you can concentrate your power. It will also make it easier to nurture it with positive energy, which you'll receive back with the help of Oshun. Remember to keep your altar clean, both physically and spiritually. The easiest way to do both is to cover it with a large piece of yellow cloth when you aren't using it. Occasionally, you can remove everything, clean the dust and other debris from the surface, and put everything back on the altar. Make sure you cleanse it regularly with incense or smudging to dispel negative influences, as these can interfere when it comes time to communicate with Oshun. Pay attention to the goddess's clues regarding the offerings she wants to receive. Sometimes, she will tell you exactly what to prepare next or what tools to use.

Chapter 7: Spells and Rituals for Love and Beauty

Now that you've learned about Oshun correspondences, you'll be ready to try them out in spells and rites dedicated to the goddess. This chapter is about love chants, baths, rituals, and other work that can enhance your natural beauty by healing you from the inside out. Using Oshun's correspondences, you can attract new love, strengthen the love you already have, and empower yourself with confidence and strength.

It's important to focus on love and beauty when creating these rituals.
https://unsplash.com/photos/lH973Qz0Iy4

Oshun's Self-Care Ritual

Oshun is known for her benevolent and caring nature, and she can inspire you to take better care of yourself. The colors of the tools used in the ritual, including the sunflower, pumpkin, and honey, are all associated with the power of the love goddess, which you can harness through this ritual.

Ingredients:

- A statute or picture of Oshun
- Sunflower petals (Fresh - or dried if they aren't in season.)
- 1 pumpkin
- 1 large yellow candle
- 1 piece of a brown paper bag (Or any brown, yellow, or gold recycled material.)
- 1 pen
- A few drops of honey
- Yellow, gold, or copper jewelry
- Yellow fruits if they're in season; if not, orange ones work as well

Instructions:

1. Place the yellow candle in front of the statue or picture of Oshun on your altar and light it.

2. Close your eyes, take a deep breath to calm your mind, and concentrate on your intention. Repeat it in your mind a couple of times and, if needed, say it out loud to solidify it.

3. Pour a few drops of honey into a container you've placed beside the candle. Arrange the yellow fruit and jewelry around the candle, honey, and representation to make the offering.

4. Open your eyes, set the pumpkin in front of you, and make a round opening on its top.

5. On the piece of paper, write your intention down. Fold the paper and place it inside the pumpkin.

6. Take the candle, tip it, and pour the wax on top of the paper. The wax will seal the opening in the pumpkin too.

7. Repeat your intention before putting out the candle.

8. If you can, take the pumpkin to the nearest river or sweet water source and offer it to Oshun.

If you need to reiterate your intention or require more time to get empowered through Oshun, you can relight the candle and repeat your intent any time you want during the following five days.

Sour Bath to Empower Yourself Mentally

The purpose of this bath is to acknowledge that while negative energies are currently affecting you, positive influences are just waiting for you to invite them. Immersing yourself in this sour bath made from bitter herbs will help you deal with the negativity in and around you and dispel it, all while boosting your mood.

Ingredients:

- A cup
- 7 drops of ammonia
- A few tea light candles
- 1/2 cup of vinegar
- Sunflowers and other yellow, orange, and white flowers
- Fresh or dried bitter herbs, such as dandelion, yarrow, horehound, wormwood, and stinging nettle

Instructions:

1. Start this ritual before sunset by filling up your bathtub with hot water. Adjust the temperature to how you usually like it.

2. Carefully arrange and light the tea light candles around the bathtub's rim. Leave enough room between at least two of the candles. You'll need this space to safely enter and exit the tub.

3. When the water in the tub has reached the desired level, turn off the artificial lights in your bathroom.

4. Toss the rest of the ingredients into the bathwater, then enter the tub between two candles.

5. As you immerse yourself in the water and inhale the bitter scent of the herbs, focus on the different aspects of your life to see if there is hidden negativity in any of them.

6. If you require additional guidance, you can ask Oshun to help you overcome any bitter experiences.

7. Aim to spend a total of seven minutes immersed in the water, so make sure you dip your head into the water from time to time.

8. Once your bathwater starts to cool, exit the tub through the same gap between the same candles you entered through.

9. Scoop some of your bathwater into the cup - along with the ingredients.

10. Drain the tub while you let yourself dry naturally so the beneficial effects of the herbs can soak into your skin.

11. Put on dark clothes, and take the cup with the bathwater outside.

12. Face east, hold the cup over your head, and chant:

   "I have now handed the goddess her due.

   I now ask her to hold onto me.

   With this water, I cast out all the negative energies from my life. Ashé, ashé!"

13. Toss out the water from the cup, return to your home, and reflect on your strengths.

14. Drink lots of room-temperature water after the bath to replenish the fluids you lost while soaking.

You can include this bath in your regular pampering and healthcare practice. Apply Shea butter or other natural moisturizing agents afterward so the herbs can take a better effect. Instead of using electronics right after your bath, spend your time doing mindfulness exercises instead.

Bath for Attracting Positive Energy

Once you've dispelled the negative influences from your life, you'll need to replace them with positive energy. This will help you find the love (starting from self-love), confidence, and strength you need. Take this bath at sunrise to cleanse and revitalize your body. The ingredients, like milk, eggs, and honey, are Oshun's favorite - and they will nourish your body and invigorate your mind anytime you need some pampering.

Ingredients:

- A few tea light candles
- A few drops of honey
- 3 cups of milk
- 1 teaspoon of ground cinnamon
- 1 teaspoon of ground nutmeg
- Flowers with all-white petals, such as roses, lilies, white chrysanthemums, and daisies
- Sunflowers
- Five different fresh or dried herbs with invigorating effects, such as angelica, hyssop, allspice, and comfrey
- Cocoa or Shea butter (optional)
- 1 raw egg
- 1 cup
- Your favorite perfume

Instructions:

1. Shortly before sunrise, fill your bathtub with hot water.
2. Carefully arrange the tea light candles around the tub's rim as instructed in the previous recipe and light them.
3. When the bathtub is full enough, turn off the water and all the other lights in the bathroom.
4. Crack the egg and toss it into the water. It may start to cook a little bit, but this is normal.
5. Throw in the flowers, herbs, and cinnamon, followed by the nutmeg, milk, and honey.
6. Add a few drops of your favorite perfume, and gently stir the water to evenly distribute all the ingredients.
7. Enter the tub through the gap between two candles.
8. When you enter the water, focus on the positive aspects of your life. Consider all the good experiences you had on that day.
9. It's a good idea to express your gratitude to Oshun for all the blessings you've received so far.

10. Aim to spend 7 minutes completely immersed in the water, so make sure you dip your head under the water from time to time.

11. Once the water starts to cool, exit the tub through the same gap you entered through.

12. Scoop some of your bathwater into the cup along with the ingredients.

13. Drain your tub while you let yourself dry naturally instead of using a towel so the effect of the herbs can soak into your skin.

14. Put on light-colored clothes, and take the cup with the bathwater outside.

15. Face east, hold the cup over your head, and recite:

> *"I welcome all the positive energies into my life that await me on my path!*
>
> *As I toss this water where it's needed the most,*
>
> *I ask the goddess Oshun to bless me with health, love, and happiness! Ashé, ashé!"*

16. Toss out the water, go back inside, and get ready to welcome the blessings you've invoked.

Like in the previous bath, you can incorporate this bath into your regular beauty and healthcare routine. Aim to meditate, journey, or perform any other form of self-care after bathing and heading out for the day. However, if you don't have time for these, don't worry. Avoiding using electronics and having calm thoughts right after your bath can still help you remain positive throughout the day and attract more positive energy.

Ritual Love Bath

Since Oshun is the patroness of love, she can make your wishes come true regarding matters of the heart. Instead of using a yellow candle, this rite uses a white candle. This ensures that you can see clearly and don't overlook the person intended for you. Using your favorite perfume will attract them to your side.

Ingredients:

- 5 sunflower petals
- 1 large bowl

- 1 white candle
- A few drops of honey
- A statute or symbol of Oshun
- A pinch of ground cinnamon
- Your favorite perfume

Instructions:

1. Place the white candle in front of the representation of the goddess on your altar and light it.

2. Tell Oshun about your desire to attract love into your life. If possible, say it out loud.

3. Place the sunflower petals in a bowl, drizzle them with honey, and sprinkle cinnamon on top. Lastly, add a few spritzes of your favorite perfume.

4. Cover the ingredients with water and let them soak for a few minutes.

5. Take a shower or a bath, and slowly pour the contents of the bowl over your body. Start at your neck and slowly move toward your feet.

6. Close your eyes and repeat your intention once again silently.

The candle should be only lit when you have time to supervise it. You can ignite it any time during the following 5 consecutive days. The bath, on the other hand, should only be repeated once every 2-3 weeks to leave enough time for love to find its way into your life.

Spell to Strengthen Your Love

This spell is perfect for strengthening love and waking up passion in a romantic relationship. The spell should be enacted on Oshun's sacred day, Friday, for the best effects. It's an incredibly popular spell among Santeria practitioners.

Ingredients:

- 5 different types of alcoholic beverages
- 1 coconut
- 1 tablespoon of molasses
- 1 tablespoon of honey

- 1 tablespoon of brown sugar
- 1 tablespoon of white sugar
- 1 yellow candle
- 1 yellow ribbon

Instructions:

1. Break the coconut down the middle, remove half the water, and put that aside.
2. Add a tablespoon of each beverage and the rest of the ingredients, then pour the other half of the water back into the coconut.
3. Close the two halves of the coconut by pressing them together and tying them with the yellow ribbon.
4. Place the coconut in front of the candle on your altar.
5. Light the candle and ask Oshun to help you strengthen the love in your relationship.
6. Repeat the last step for 5 nights, lighting the candle each time. Leave it lit while making your inquiry and saying a quick prayer of gratitude.

Love Potion with Jasmine, Rose, and Cinnamon

By using this love potion, you can improve your relationship and boost your mood. Due to its blood-regulating properties, cinnamon increases passion and lets you enjoy your relationship even more. Jasmine and rose are both associated with sensuality. They also cause euphoria and reduce anxiety which would hinder the development of your relationship.

Ingredients:

- 1 tablespoon of dried rose petals
- 2 tablespoons of dried jasmine flowers
- ¼ teaspoon of vanilla extract
- 1 cup of fresh water
- 2 cinnamon sticks

Instructions:

1. Pour a cup of water into a pot. You can use more for a stronger effect or less for a softer potion.

2. Add the remaining ingredients to the water and stir until well combined.

3. Bring the mixture to a boil and simmer for 2-3 minutes.

4. Remove the mixture from the heat.

5. Let the potion cool, then consume as needed. Drink with a little sparkling water whenever you feel stuck in your relationship or need to stir up passion.

6. You can leave the mixture in the fridge in an airtight container for 5-7 days.

Spell for Enhancing Your Beauty

If you would like to enhance your attractiveness and gain a little more confidence, this spell will be the perfect tool for it. You can use it alongside any ritual you do to communicate with Oshun, including meditation, or even when saying a simple prayer of gratitude for her blessings.

Ingredients:

- 5 yellow candles (or 3 yellow and 2 white ones)
- A few drops of rose essential oil
- 1 piece of yellow tape or thread
- Offerings for the goddess
- Representations of Oshun (status and common symbols such as gold coins, shells, feathers, etc.)
- Sunflower petals, your favorite incense, music, or anything else that can put you in a good mood

Instructions:

1. Prepare all the ingredients and place them in front of you on your altar or sacred place.

2. This is optional, but if you want to, you can take a soothing bath beforehand (you can take one of the baths described above) to ensure your body and mind will be relaxed enough to focus on the spell.

3. Make sure you don't get distracted, and set the room temperature to slightly warm. Feel free to put on sensual clothes or, if you prefer, anything you feel the most comfortable wearing.

4. Get into a comfortable position in front of your sacred space.

5. Place the candles on the edges of the altar and light them. Scatter the sunflower petals and the representation of the goddess around the candles.

6. Place the symbol of Oshun in front of the offerings you've prepared.

7. Take a few relaxing breaths and start focusing on your intention. Exclude anything else from your mind.

8. Take the piece of yellow thread and start rolling it around the index finger of your dominant hand. While you're doing this, recite the following:

   "I see myself as a vision of beauty as I am now full of confidence.

   I'm filled with love, passion, and warmth, and my face is ever-graceful.

   Everyone will notice how attractive I am now, inside and out.

   And I will soon find someone who appreciates what lies beyond my beauty."

9. Close your eyes and repeat the chant in your head. Keep twisting the thread around your finger until you're ready to open your eyes.

10. Tie the thread to the base of one of the candles but remain in the same position. Visualize your newfound attractiveness and being full of confidence and inner strength.

11. Look into the candlelight, and let it fill you with all the self-confidence, energy, and grace you need to find the happiness you deserve.

12. Focus on this intention as long as possible. When you feel ready, eat and drink from the offerings you've prepared for the goddess. Sharing the meal with her symbolically will prompt her to help you faster.

13. When you're ready to finish, blow out the candles and take the thread with you. You can put it into your pocket or bag or wear it as a reminder of your intention and attractiveness.

Spell to Sweeten Your Relationships

With this simple spell, you can sweeten any relationship in your life. You can make anyone from your partner to your boss more receptive to your needs and become more caring toward you. It uses the sweetness of honey, although you can substitute it with sugar if you're in a hurry to get positive attention.

Ingredients:

- A bottle or a jar you don't mind discarding
- Honey, as needed
- Tap water
- Pen and paper

Instructions:

1. Add water and honey to the bottle and shake it to combine.
2. Using the paper and the pen, write the name of the person you want to sweeten toward you.
3. Place the bottle on the altar until your intention has been realized. After that, you can discard the bottle. Alternatively, you can pour the contents out and use them as sweet incense.

Chapter 8: Spells and Rituals Abundance and Prosperity

Besides love and beauty, Oshun can also help obtain prosperity and abundance in several aspects of life. Whether you wish to grow spiritually, are dealing with fertility issues, or want financial security for yourself and your loved ones, obtaining Oshun's blessings can be the key to a better life. This chapter enlists several spells and rituals designed for abundance, fertility, and even the protection of those who wish for these gifts. With the help of these tools and by building a powerful connection with the goddess, you can make your dreams come true.

Abundance and prosperity come from giving an offering to Oshun.
https://unsplash.com/photos/K0E6E0a0R3A

Prosperity Offering

Oshun is one of the best choices as an Orisha associated with prosperity. While she is often associated with abundance in relationships and spiritual wealth, you can also invoke her regarding any other area of life you want to improve. With the right combination of tools, you can have Oshun grant you material wealth and financial security.

Ingredients:

- 5 oranges
- 1 yellow candle
- 1 white plate
- Cinnamon
- Honey
- A representation of Oshun

Instructions:

1. Place the yellow candle in front of the representation of Oshun on your altar and light it.
2. Recite your intention out loud to make sure Oshun can hear you.
3. Put the oranges on a white plate and drizzle them with honey.
4. Sprinkle some cinnamon on top of the oranges as well.
5. Leave the oranges and the topping in front of the Orisha beside the candle for five days.
6. When the five days are up, you can put away the candle and dispose of the offering too.

The candle shouldn't be left burning continuously for 5 days. Ensure you snuff it out anytime you can't attend to it and light it again when you can supervise it. Also, use fresh oranges to stay safely at room temperature until the ritual is completed.

Offering for Professional Growth

The best time to make this offering to Oshun is when you're seeking a promotion or a new job. However, you can also present this at any other time throughout the year if you require her protection or guidance. Doing it at a riverbank will let Oshun know she is needed much faster. That said, you can do it through an open window if you don't have a river or other freshwater source nearby.

Ingredients:

- A statue or picture of Oshun
- A coin or money bill
- A piece of yellow cloth
- Oshun incense powder
- Cowrie shells (these are associated with divination, so you can foretell whether you're getting the new job)
- Fruit, veggies, or other offerings of your choice
- A basket

Instructions:

1. Spread the piece of cloth onto your altar and place the representation of Oshun on top of it in the center of the altar.
2. Place the money into a small bowl and pour some incense powder into another one.
3. Light the incense powder and place the shells in the basket.
4. Place all your offerings around the basket as well.
5. Light the candle and say the following prayer to Oshun:

   "I celebrate you, Oshun, the goddess of sweet waters.

   I will praise and serve you as long your waters nourish the Earth.

   Let your waters be calm - so they bring me my job.

   And I'll forever hold you in my heart. Ashé, ashé. "

6. Calm your thoughts by focusing on the flame of the candle. You can also close your eyes and meditate for a couple of minutes if you find it easier to relax your mind this way.
7. Work on manifesting your intention until the incense burns out, then express your gratitude to Oshun for the blessing she may bestow on you.

The Oshun incense powder can be substituted with another of your choice.

Oshun's Ritual for Creativity and Prosperity

You can achieve spiritual prosperity by engaging in new creative activities. If you don't know where to start your creative journey, you can ask Oshun for guidance using this ritual. Besides showing you how to express your creativity, she can also help you release all the burdens hindering you from reaching your full spiritual potential. Like many other rituals for Oshun, performing this near a river is recommended. If you don't have access to one, you can do it at the altar and symbolically send your worries downriver.

Ingredients:

- A piece of yellow or gold cloth to represent Oshun
- A jar of honey
- Spring water in a large container (if you're doing this at an inside altar inside rather than near a water source)
- A piece of sweet fruit (seasonal)
- Seeds you would plant in the spring (preferably pumpkin, sunflower, squash, or any other of Oshun's favorites
- Fresh flowers - yellow, white, and orange
- Pen and paper
- A bell
- A small basket
- Glitter and other craft material

Instructions:

1. Spread the cloth on your altar or the ground if you do this in the open.
2. Write your intention on a piece of paper, fold it, and place it into the basket.
3. While focusing on your intention, start decorating the basket with glitter and other crafting materials.
4. When you've finished, place the fruit and seeds into the basket, sprinkle them with honey and flowers, and place it into the river (or water container).

5. Ring the bell to call on Oshun's attention and say a prayer of gratitude for her blessings.

Fertility Ritual

This traditional Yoruba ritual has been used by young women who want to conceive a child. Apart from this, Oshun may grant you fertility in many other aspects of life, such as art, work, and even cultivating relationships. The colors and seeds of the pumpkin symbolize the power of nature's fertility.

Ingredients:

- 1 melon
- 1 yellow candle
- Paper and pen
- A representation of the goddess

Instructions:

1. Place the yellow candle in front of the representation of Oshun on your altar and light it.
2. Close your eyes and focus on manifesting your wishes. Saying them out loud often helps.
3. Open your eyes, take the pen, and write your wishes down on the paper.
4. Place the piece of paper on top of the melon. Then, hold it on your stomach (if you want to conceive), in front of your heart (if you want fertility in your relationships, or on your head (for productivity in work, hobbies, or art).
5. Repeat your wishes and ask the goddess to help you realize them.
6. When you feel your wishes have been heard, take the melon to the nearest water source and offer it to Oshun. Alternatively, you can bury it in your garden or eat it within a day or two.

You may leave the candle burning briefly after the ritual is completed. Still, if you are likely to leave it unattended, it's best to snuff it out. You can relight the candle any time you wish during the next five days.

5-Day Candle Ritual for Oshun

Calling on Oshun can be helpful when you need to eliminate bad luck from your life and replace it with good fortune. A large yellow candle will ensure you acquire the abundance you desire. The addition of the yellow food will appease Oshun, so she lends you the ashe you need to obtain your goals.

Using a large, yellow candle brings abundance.
https://unsplash.com/photos/66qsl7ia2cE

Ingredients:

- A piece of yellow cotton yarn or thread
- Yellow and white flowers - fresh or dry
- Sweet potatoes
- Coconut shavings
- Honey
- Pumpkin seeds
- A large yellow candle
- A representation of Oshun

Instructions:

1. Organize your altar or sacred space by clearing up anything you won't need for this ritual.

2. Place the yellow candle and the symbol representing Oshun in the middle of your altar.

3. Prepare the sweet potatoes, pumpkin seeds, coconut shavings, and honey in separate bowls and place those on the altar.

4. If you're using chopped dry flowers, sprinkle them around the candle and tie the yellow yarn or thread around the bottom of the candle.

5. If you're using fresh or whole dried flowers, tie them in a bunch with the yarn or thread.

6. When you are ready, light the candle, close your eyes and prepare to call on Oshun.

   Then, recite the following chant:

   "Oh, powerful Oshun, please lend me your strength,

   Send me luck and fortune.

   May I be strong and wise,

   So, I can obtain prosperity.

   Help me stay loving and caring,

   And keep treating others with the same integrity."

Traditionally, the candle was intended to be left burning 5 days and nights after saying the prayer. However, this is generally not recommended due to safety concerns. Not to mention that, like many other spells, this one works only as long as you maintain a fierce focus on your intention. No matter how eager you are to obtain prosperity, you'll only be able to concentrate on this for a short period of time. Because of this, it's better to burn the candle for several minutes over 5 days. Whenever you have time during the day, light the candle, and recite the spell. When you've finished, snuff it out and go about your day. When you can, relight it once again until it burns out. The food is supposed to be served raw, but Oshun will also accept your offering if you prepare a dish from the above-mentioned food sources - especially if you eat alongside her.

Ritual for Fertility and Protection

This ritual can serve as both a tool for resolving fertility issues and protecting expectant mothers and their families. It uses Oshun's ultimate fertility symbol, the pumpkin, along with plenty of her other associations. They can help you ward off the negative influences causing fertility issues or threatening the safety of a pregnant mother, their baby, and their family. This ritual can be performed by pregnant women, their female family members, friends, or even the unborn child's father. You can combine this rite with other purification or protection rituals, including cleansing baths and self-care routines.

Ingredients:

- 1 medium-sized pumpkin
- 1 white plate
- A handful of patchouli roots
- Sunflowers and other yellow flowers (Life Everlasting is particularly recommended for this purpose)
- Honey, as needed
- Orange essential oil, as needed
- 1 yellow candle
- A few drops of your favorite lotion or soap
- A statue or picture of the goddess, Orisha, or saint (depending on how you wish to celebrate her)
- A bell
- A beaded necklace or bracelet in Oshun's colors
- 5 gold coins (regular coins work too if you can't find gold ones)
- Yellow and gold glitter to represent the goddess, as these are her favorites
- Silver and white glitter for stability
- Blue glitter for harmony
- Red glitter for passion and success for the mother and the child
- 1 Glass of water (river or tap water)
- 1 Glass of white wine or champagne (optional)

Instructions:

1. Place the white plate in the middle of your altar, right in front of the representation of Oshun.

2. Sprinkle some dried patchouli and flower petals on the plate, and place your pumpkin on top. If you wish (and if you're the one who is expecting or wanting to conceive), you can hold the pumpkin in front of your heart or stomach and quickly say your intention before placing the pumpkin on the plate.

3. Place the yellow candle on the right of the plate, and light it. You can anoint it beforehand with orange essential oil.

4. Put the cup of water or wine on the left side of the plate, next to the bell.

5. Pour some lotion, orange essential oil, and honey on the top of the pumpkin. Use your hands to cover the entire pumpkin generously with these wonderful liquids. While you do, say your intention, and ask for Oshun's blessings.

6. Use the bell to get Oshun's attention before moving on to the next step.

7. Once you've got her attention, you can retain it by sprinkling the glitters on the top of the pumpkin.

8. After anointing it with the liquids, place the necklace or bracelet on top of the pumpkin.

9. Place the 5 coins on the plate around the pumpkin. If your pumpkin is large and you don't have much space around it, you can place the coins on top of it, around its stem.

10. Raise your glass in the name of Oshun as you recite a prayer of gratitude for the blessings you're about to receive.

Suppose you're working in a closed space. In that case, you can leave everything on the altar (after snuffing out the candle, of course) for 1-2 days, depending on the room's temperature. After that, remove the plate with the pumpkin, but you can leave the rest. Gently wash the bracelet and place it on the representation of Oshun. Say a prayer to it every day while you wait for the blessings.

Oshun Protection and Luck Spell

If you feel down on your luck, this spell can manifest Oshun's blessings. They can come in the form of good luck, an abundance of fortune, or simply having better experiences in life. The spell will also provide you with the protection you need from those who will envy your success once luck returns to your side. You can combine it with other prosperity rituals and prayers.

Ingredients:

- 1 yellow candle
- Your favorite incense
- Honey, as needed
- A piece of parchment paper
- Money (paper bill)
- Natural soap (with honey, sugar, honeysuckle, or other sweet natural ingredients)
- A few drops of magnet oil (optional, you can use a magnet instead) to attract fortune
- 1 black crystal (for example, jet) for luck, protection, and money
- A skipping river rock (or another representation of a river)
- A picture or statute of Oshun
- 1 small red candle for making the intention into reality as soon as possible
- 1 small gold candle for success
- 1 small yellow candle to help communicate your wishes
- 1 bell
- A pinch of dried chrysanthemum, marigold, and rose petals to keep things going once you've got your luck
- Bee pollen, as needed

Instructions:

1. Start by writing your request on parchment paper and join the paper with the money bill.

2. In your hands, mix a few drops of soap and magnet oil. Gently cover the paper and the money with the mixture.

3. Place the paper and the money on the altar, and put the river rock and black crystal on top of it or next to it, depending on how the rocks are shaped. If they're too large and round, you can place them next to the paper to prevent them from rolling off.

4. Tell Oshun what you wish for and say a prayer of gratitude. You can use the bell to get her attention.

5. Place the large yellow candle next to the paper and money and light it.

6. Sprinkle some chrysanthemums, marigolds, and roses around the candle and put a little aside for a bath.

7. Sprinkle a little bee pollen around the candle. Alternatively, you can also anoint the candle with honey.

8. Prepare your bathwater with honey, bee pollen, herbs, and natural soap. While preparing your bath, write an intention for each small candle.

9. After taking your bath, return to your altar and light the smaller candles while making your intention known for one final time.

10. Take the skipping rock or other representation of a river to your nearest water source, along with some honey, and say a prayer of gratitude for the blessing you'll receive. Keep the black stone with you as a talisman or reminder of your intention.

If needed, you can recite your intention several times. You don't need to take the cleansing bath every time, but you can call Oshun with the bell to remind her of your wishes. Alternatively, you can use 3 small candles of the same color if you have a specific request to reinforce. For safety reasons, snuff out the large candle while you're taking a bath, and relight it along with smaller ones once you've returned to the altar.

Chapter 9: Holy Days and Festivals

The celebrations of Oshun, known as Holy Days and Festivals, are an essential aspect of honoring the Goddess. However, many devotees may be uncertain about what these celebrations entail, when to observe them, and how to properly honor Oshun during these events. Therefore, educating oneself on Oshun's traditional ceremonies, rituals, and practices is crucial. By gaining knowledge of the origins and cultural background of each Festival, practitioners can deepen their understanding of Oshun's power and her role in everyday life. Continue reading to learn more about the Festivals related to Oshun and the best ways to celebrate them with respect and reverence for the Goddess.

Festivals allow people to celebrate and praise Oshun.
https://www.maxpixel.net/The-Art-Of-Man-Africa-Music-Culture-The-Festival-3644226

Osun-Osogbo Festival

The Osun-Osogbo Festival is a highly popular and significant traditional festival celebrated in Osogbo, the capital of Osun State, Nigeria. It has been held annually for centuries by the people of Osun State. The festival is dedicated to the goddess Osun, who is believed by the people of this area to be responsible for fertility and prosperity.

The celebration begins around August 1 to 29th each year and features a variety of events such as parades, music and dance performances, masquerading rituals, and spiritual invocations. The highlight of the festival is when devotees visit the riverbank shrine of Osoogun, located along the River Osun, to make sacrifices to their ancestors and seek blessings from the River Goddess.

Oshun is an Orisha, or goddess associated with love, fertility, beauty, gold, abundance, and diplomacy. This Yoruba deity is revered in many religions as a bringer of peace and prosperity to her devotees. During the Osun-Osogbo Festival, people gather to honor Oshun through celebration and prayer.

In Nigeria, one of the largest celebrations occurs in Osogbo city, where thousands of people come together to participate in processions often accompanied by music. People decorate their homes with colorful fabrics, ornaments, and banners to mark the occasion. During the processions, people pray and make offerings in honor of Oshun.

In Ghana, the festival is commonly known as Osun Festival. It is celebrated in the same way as it is in Nigeria, but with a greater emphasis on traditional activities such as drumming, dancing, and storytelling. These activities are believed to unite the community and are an important part of the celebration. The festival is also a time for families to come together and give thanks for the blessings that Oshun has bestowed upon them.

In Benin, the festival is known as the Igue Festival. It is celebrated similarly to Nigeria, focusing on traditional activities such as dancing and drumming. The festival is also a time for the community to come together and give thanks to Oshun for her blessings.

In Latin America, the festival is celebrated in honor of Yemaya – the equivalent of Oshun in the Yoruba religion. The celebrations tend to focus more on water rituals such as bathing in rivers or seas to cleanse oneself of any spiritual impurities. This is believed to bring balance and harmony to the individual and their community and is seen as an important aspect of the celebration.

Overall, the Igue Festival is an important celebration deeply rooted in the history and culture of Benin and celebrated in other African countries and Latin America. It is a time for the community to come together and give thanks.

The festival culminates on August 31st with the traditional Osun-Osogbo procession. This procession is an important ritual in which worshippers walk from the sacred grove of Osoogun to Osogbo town, carrying a statue of their goddess and singing her praises. In the evening, a grand finale is held at the palace of the Ataoja (king), where all those who participated in the procession are honored.

The best way to celebrate an Oshun Festival at home is by creating a sacred space dedicated to honoring her. This could include setting up an altar and decorating it with offerings like fruits or coins. Other activities include singing traditional songs in her honor and performing special dances or rituals that celebrate her divine presence. You can also get creative and make your own festivities by organizing a potluck dinner or gathering of friends where you can share stories about Oshun and exchange tokens of appreciation for her blessings.

No matter where you are in the world, the Osun-Osogbo Festival is a great reminder to appreciate the beauty and power of nature. By celebrating this festival, people honor their ancestors and their shared humanity.

Oshun River Festival

The Oshun River Festival is a vibrant celebration of the Yoruba goddess Oshun, held annually in Osogbo, Nigeria. The festival, which typically takes place over three days in September, is a time for devotees to pay homage to Oshun through traditional worship practices, music, and dance performances.

At the heart of the festival is the main event, which takes place at a shrine located near the banks of the Osun River, dedicated to Oshun. Here, devotees gather to offer prayers, make offerings of food, flowers, and other items, and participate in rituals for blessings from the goddess. After these ceremonies, the festivities begin with lively drumming and dancing around bonfires, celebrating Oshun's presence.

The festival's second day is dedicated to traditional worship practices, including ceremonies for cleansing the body and spirit. These activities occur in shrines and sacred spaces throughout Osogbo, such as Olumo Rock and Opa Oranmiyan Shrine. Parades also feature colorful floats, musicians playing traditional African instruments, and people dressed in vibrant ceremonial costumes singing and dancing in praise of Oshun.

On the final day of celebrations, processions lead people through different parts of the town to visit sites associated with Oshun's history before returning to the main shrine to present offerings and give thanks to the goddess. The festivities continue late into the night, with food being shared among families and friends as they exchange stories about past festivals.

The Oshun River Festival is a time of joyous celebration, recognizing the connection between humanity and divinity. It provides an opportunity for participants to express gratitude and connect with their goddess through devotional acts in her honor.

Igue Festival

The Igue Festival is an annual five-day celebration occurring in Uselu, Benin City, Nigeria, from October 28th to November 2nd. It is a time of great joy and celebration for worshippers of the Yoruba goddess Oshun as they gather to honor and pay homage to her. The festival is deeply rooted in the history and culture of Benin and has been celebrated for centuries.

On the festival's first day, participants gather at the shrine of Oshun to decorate it with flowers and white cloths, make offerings of thanksgiving, and petition for blessings. Traditional music and dancing then begin as people give thanks and praise to Oshun. Throughout the five days of celebrations, there are parties, parades, performances by dancers and masqueraders, feasts of delicious foods, singing competitions between groups or villages, traditional ceremonies such as blessing children with water from Oshun's sacred river Obo Osebo, storytelling sessions by elders sharing ancient stories about Oshun's power over life on earth, and cultural art displays including weaving baskets with natural dyes.

At night during the festival, special rituals are held under the moonlight to bring about luck for individuals or families who have made offerings to Oshun. These rituals can include pouring specially prepared water over pieces of cloth laid out around shrines, representing different types of fortune or wishes that may be granted by Oshun, such as health or prosperity.

For those unable to attend the Igue Festival in Uselu, there are still ways to participate in the celebration from home. One popular method is dedicating a day or two to prayer, specifically honoring Oshun and her power over life on Earth. One could also incorporate herbs associated with Oshun, such as rosemary or basil, into meals while offering silent prayers of thanksgiving for all that Oshun has done in their lives. This allows for a personal and spiritual connection to the festival, even if physically absent from the celebrations.

The Igue Festival is integral to Benin City culture, passed down through generations since ancient times. It provides a unique opportunity to connect with history and celebrate one's faith in a vibrant atmosphere. Each year in October and November, thousands gather in Uselu, regardless of religious differences, to honor Oshun.

During the festival, devotees participate in various rituals and ceremonies steeped in tradition and symbolism. They make offerings to Oshun, such as fruits, sweets, and flowers, to show their gratitude for her blessings. They also participate in traditional dances and drumming to invoke the goddess' presence and connect with her energy. Many people also visit the various shrines and sacred sites in the area dedicated to Oshun, where they can give thanks and seek her guidance. Overall, the Igue Festival serves as an important reminder of Oshun's enduring power and the Yoruba people's deep cultural roots.

Oshala Festival

The Oshala Festival is an annual celebration occurring in December, honoring the Yoruba river goddess Oshun. It is a time of prayer and thanksgiving, where devotees offer sacrifices and offerings to Oshun to obtain healing and protection. The festival is celebrated at various locations throughout Nigeria, typically near rivers or other sources of water. The dates of the festival vary each year based on the lunar cycle but generally fall within a two-week period leading up to December 31st. In some areas, celebrations may last up to three weeks, beginning on the full moon closest to December 21st.

It is particularly renowned in riverside communities such as Osogbo, Ijebu-Ode, and Ilesa. During the festival, participants make offerings of fruits, grains, and other ceremonial items at shrines near water sources to ensure that Oshun's blessings reach them in abundance. They also offer prayers for healing from physical and emotional distress and protection from danger and hardship.

In addition to these traditional practices, modern-day devotees can celebrate the Oshala Festival by participating in activities such as drumming circles and dancing around sacred fires lit in honor of Oshun's spirit. Special songs are sung in her praise, and delicate gifts are presented at her shrine as tokens of respect and appreciation for all that she has done for them.

For those who cannot attend the local festivities, it is still possible to honor Oshun's spirit at home by adorning living spaces with yellow cloths (representative of Oshun's color) or making small offerings at an altar dedicated specifically to her divinity. Candles and incense can also be lit, symbolizing the connection between humanity and nature to ensure that blessings reach those who are far away from any celebration site.

The Oshala Festival is a time-honored tradition celebrated in Nigeria for centuries. It is an annual two-week celebration, usually leading up to New Year's Eve, during which devotees of the Yoruba river goddess Oshun come together to express their gratitude and honor her divine grace. This festival is deeply rooted in the cultural and spiritual heritage of the Yoruba people. It is a celebration not just of the goddess but also of the devotion and dedication of those who have honored her for generations. The festival is marked by elaborate ceremonies, traditional music and dancing, offerings, and feasts, all in honor of Oshun and her powerful presence in the lives of her followers.

Elegba Festival

Elegba Festival is an annual celebration that honors the powerful Orisha Elegba and the Yoruba deity Oshun in Nigeria. Held every February at the Ile-Ife Palace in Osun state, the festival is a time for offering prayers and offerings to Oshun, the goddess associated with love, fertility, beauty, wealth, and prosperity. The festival includes offerings of food, drink, flowers, and other items to Oshun, as well as traditional Yoruba music and dance performances.

The festival typically takes place in February, with the dates varying from year to year. The event begins with a procession carrying offerings to Orisha Elegba, followed by a series of rituals and ceremonies honoring Oshun. Traditional music and dance performances pay homage to both Orisha Elegba and Oshun during this time.

At the Ile-Ife Palace, people gather to celebrate and offer their prayers and offerings to Oshun in an atmosphere of joyous singing, dancing, and feasting. Local markets are also present, where people can buy gifts for friends or loved ones or simply participate in the vibrant atmosphere permeating the palace grounds during the festival.

The celebrations don't end at the Ile-Ife Palace, as many communities across Nigeria have their own celebrations that honor Orisha Elegba, featuring colorful parades with dancers costumed as animals and wearing elaborate masks depicting different gods or goddesses such as Oshun. Traditional drumming and acrobatics also add an extra layer of enjoyment to these festivities.

Those who cannot attend the festival in person can still participate by offering prayers or burning incense to honor Orisha Elegba and Oshun before images representing them both. Special meals or drinks can also be prepared in their honor, allowing you to be a part of this sacred annual tradition even from a distance.

Ultimately, Elegba Festival provides an opportunity for people to come together in celebration while also honoring one of the most important deities in Yoruba culture, Oshun. The festival brings people together spiritually, and whether they are participating in large parades or intimate home gatherings, it is sure to bring people closer together no matter where they are

Holy days

Osunseya or Ironmole Day

Osunseya, or Ironmole Day, is an annual celebration honoring the Yoruba goddess of love and fertility, Oshun. Held on the last Saturday of August, devotees celebrate the festival both in Nigeria and other parts of West Africa. The day is dedicated to Oshun's power to bring people abundance, prosperity, and fertility. It is a time for reflection on the goddess's message of love and harmony.

The celebrations usually occur in riverside villages, where devotees gather by candlelight around a shrine devoted to Oshun. They offer prayers and sacrifices, such as honey, eggs, fruits, jewelry, and animals. Many wear yellow clothing, said to please Oshun more than any other color. Traditional dances and cultural activities are also a part of the festivities.

At sunset, small boats filled with candles are lit and released into the water to symbolize hope for good fortune in the coming year. Afterward, a bonfire is lit, which is said to connect humanity directly with divinity through its flames. Families enjoy a feast as a thanksgiving offering to their protective deity.

Osunseya, or Ironmole Day, is an important annual celebration among followers of Yoruba mythology and an opportunity to renew their commitment to living better lives rooted in spirituality, kindness, love, and respect towards nature. The festival is a time for coming together to honor Oshun and a reminder of the timeless messages of love and harmony that the goddess represents.

Fridays

Every Friday, the Yoruba religion of Nigeria celebrates Oshun, a beloved deity known for her vibrant energy, creativity, and kindness. Devotees pay homage to the goddess through rituals that involve offerings of food, drink, and other gifts, dressed in yellow and white clothes to represent the sun and purity.

The celebration begins with prayer and singing at sacred sites or shrines dedicated to Oshun. Offerings of fruits, eggs, cornmeal, milk, honey, and sugar are presented to the goddess as a way of expressing gratitude and asking for blessings. After invoking the goddess's presence, devotees proceed to dance around bonfires while holding on to a white cloth, symbolizing their faith in Oshun.

For those who cannot attend the physical celebrations, it is still possible to honor Oshun at home by setting up an altar dedicated to the goddess. This can include items such as flowers, yellow candles, and river stones as offerings, along with foods associated with Oshun, such as honey cakes, mangoes, or millet porridge.

The celebration is also an opportunity for reflection and introspection, not only on one's personal life but also on the interconnectedness of all things. By embracing these beliefs and values, followers can create a harmonious space within their homes and ultimately lead themselves toward freedom from suffering and experience true bliss.

Oshun's Birthday

Oshun's Birthday is a revered and highly-anticipated annual celebration in the Yoruba religion, marking the birthday of Oshun, the goddess of love, pleasure, and fertility. This sacred day is celebrated on the 5th of April. It is steeped in tradition and historical significance, having been observed for thousands of years.

Devotees honor Oshun on her special day by performing rituals and ceremonies that involve making offerings and giving thanks for her blessings. These offerings may include flowers, sweet treats, or even animal sacrifices to express gratitude for the goddess's divine gifts and seek her protection and guidance.

In addition to traditional rituals, many followers also celebrate Oshun's Birthday in the comfort of their own homes with their loved ones. This may include hosting small gatherings where they give thanks to the goddess, enjoying sweet treats and traditional foods prepared in her honor, and dressing up in traditional clothing or adorning themselves with jewelry associated with Oshun.

It is believed that those who properly observe Oshun's Birthday will be blessed with good health, prosperity, love, joy, and harmony in life. Therefore, this special day is an essential opportunity to connect with the goddess and bring spiritual balance to one's life. Whether through traditional rituals or personal celebrations, honoring Oshun on her birthday is a powerful and meaningful way to show devotion and seek blessings.

Chapter 10: Daily Rituals to Honor Oshun

Honoring the Yoruba goddess Oshun is a wonderful way to show appreciation for her blessings. To make this daily ritual meaningful, connecting with Oshun through simple acts of kindness and generosity can be rewarding. While she is the African goddess of love, beauty, and sensuality, Oshun is also associated with fertility, abundance, and fresh water. How can one honor her in a meaningful way? This chapter will explore some creative daily rituals. From cleansing baths to affirmations of love, these rituals can promote healing and renewal. By committing to a regular practice, you are honoring her and inviting more of the supportive energy of this benevolent deity into your life.

Daily Rituals

1. Offerings

Honoring Oshun through daily offerings is important to building a relationship with the goddess and receiving her favor. These offerings are a way to show your gratitude and appreciation for all that she has done for those who love her and to ask for her blessings and guidance in your daily life.

Traditional offerings to Oshun include honey, yellow flowers, and yellow cornmeal, which are believed to have special significance for the goddess. Honey symbolizes sweetness and prosperity and is often associated with the goddess's ability to bring abundance to life. Yellow flowers, such as marigolds and sunflowers, are believed to represent joy and sunshine and are often used to invoke the goddess's blessings of happiness and positivity. Yellow cornmeal is a staple food in many African countries, is believed to represent nourishment and sustenance, and is often used to ask the goddess for her blessings of health and well-being.

Cooked rice sweetened with honey or sugar is also a common offering. Fruits such as apples, oranges, mangoes, and coconuts can also be offered, each representing different qualities associated with the goddess. For example, oranges are believed to represent joy and fertility, while coconuts are believed to represent nourishment and protection.

Yellow and gold flowers are popular choices for offerings to Oshun, as they correspond with the goddess's color associations. Still, any type of flower can be used depending on the intent of the offering. For example, tulips are believed to symbolize prosperity, while roses symbolize love and gratitude. Incense, such as cinnamon and jasmine, are also great ways to honor Oshun, as they have deep spiritual connections to her energy. They can be used to create a calming and meditative atmosphere and to invoke the goddess's presence.

Finally, simple offerings such as a glass of water or honey can also be made to show respect and ask for her blessings and guidance. These offerings can be placed on an altar dedicated to Oshun and can be accompanied by prayers or chants. By making daily offerings to Oshun, devotees can deepen their connection to the goddess and receive her blessings in their lives.

2. Meditation

Self-reflection and meditation are important aspects of honoring the goddess, Oshun. By clearing your mind and focusing on connecting with divine energy, you can deepen your connection to the goddess and receive her blessings.

When meditating in honor of Oshun, focus on visualizing her golden light within you and surrounding you, bringing balance and harmony into your life. Oshun is a powerful African goddess of love, beauty, and fertility; meditating in her honor can be a transformative experience.

To set up your daily meditation for Oshun, find a peaceful location near the water or create an artificial body of water by filling a shallow bowl with fresh spring water. Place the bowl before you and light white candles on either side. You can set up a small altar for Oshun in the area where you meditate. Place items representing her, such as gold jewelry, coins, flowers, or food offerings, such as oranges and honey. If you can burn incense, use scents like jasmine and orange blossom, which are associated with Oshun's energy.

Sit comfortably on a chair with your back straight, feet flat on the ground, hands resting palms-up on your knees, and eyes closed. Take several deep breaths as you relax into the moment. Visualize yourself opening up to receive unconditional love from the goddess Oshun. Imagine her light radiating from her heart and entering yours, opening it up even further. Notice how her light brings warmth into your body. As you continue to breathe deeply, consider any areas in your life where you feel limited or restricted. Affirm aloud that these areas are now open for transformation and growth through the power and grace of Oshun as you continue to breathe deeply in this sacred space dedicated to her energy.

When you are ready, focus on your breath and repeat mantras in honor of Oshun, such as "may I be connected to the source" or "may I have abundance in my life." Chant whatever resonates most deeply within you, such as "Oshun protect me" or "all power belongs to Oshun."

As your meditation continues, take time to visualize the blessings you want from Oshun. It could be guidance or inner peace in times of difficulty or creativity when feeling blocked. Whatever form these blessings may come in, commit them wholeheartedly to Oshun in the hope that she will hear them. After visualizing these blessings for several minutes, open your eyes and end your meditation practice with a prayer of thanksgiving for her presence in your life. Offer gratitude for all that Oshun has brought into your life so far, such as love, beauty, and fertility. Thank her for existing and being a source of nurturing energy in the universe. Express gratitude for the opportunity to receive her gifts daily if you accept them with open arms while remaining aware of personal boundaries. Allow yourself a few more moments before gently returning to physical reality, taking all the healing energy she has blessed you with today.

Once finished with your meditation practice, spend some time expressing gratitude towards Oshun for listening to your prayers and dedicating this special time to her spirit each day. Thank her for all the love, protection, and guidance that she offers to you and everyone around the world who calls upon her.

Meditating near water while honoring Oshun through mantras and prayers is a powerful way to tap into her divine energy and gain insight into your life. Oshun, the African goddess of love, beauty, and fertility, offers a wealth of knowledge, abundance, and protection to those who honor her. This daily practice helps you connect to the divine feminine energy flow and allows you to honor those who have come before you throughout history. By meditating in her honor each day, you can deepen your connection with Oshun and receive her blessings in your life.

3. Music and Dance

Music and dance are powerful ways to honor the Yoruba goddess Oshun. Oshun is a goddess of love, beauty, and fertility; music and dance are powerful expressions of these qualities. The Yoruba people have long used music and dance as a way to honor their gods, including Oshun. Traditional Yoruba songs dedicated to Oshun often include prayers of gratitude or requests for blessings and are accompanied by rhythms created with drums and other percussion instruments. The dances performed for Oshun use symbolic movements to express admiration and respect for her. One such dance, "Oshoaluwo," involves stamping feet on the ground in patterns representing the goddess's power and influence over nature.

Another traditional dance that honors Oshun is the "Ebora" dance. It is a celebratory dance performed in honor of the goddess and her powers of fertility. It is usually performed by women and involves sensual, fluid movements meant to emulate the flow of water, which is closely associated with Oshun.

The "Osun Osogbo" dance is another traditional dance performed in honor of the goddess Oshun. This dance is performed during the annual Osun Osogbo Festival in Nigeria, dedicated to the goddess. The dancers wear brightly colored clothes and headdresses adorned with beads and other ornaments. They carry staffs and swords as they perform the dance. The dance combines rhythmic movements and choreography to represent the goddess's power and influence over the natural world.

In addition to these traditional dances, there are also modern interpretations of Oshun-inspired dance. For example, the "Brown Skin Girl" music video by Beyoncé, which was shot on location in Nigeria and featured traditional African clothing and cultural elements, has been seen as a modern interpretation of an Oshun-inspired dance. The video's use of movement, costuming, and imagery has been interpreted as a way of expressing admiration and respect for the goddess and her influence on women of color.

Music and dance are integral parts of Yoruba culture – and powerful ways to honor the goddess, Oshun. They serve as a means of expressing gratitude and admiration for the goddess while also connecting with her energy and power physically and spiritually.

4. Prayers and Blessings

Prayer is a meaningful way to honor the goddess Oshun and connect with her powerful energy. It can bring balance, peace, and joy into your life. To make the most of your prayers, try to recite them at sunrise or sunset, when the day and night transition, as it is a special time to thank all the gods, including Oshun, for their blessings, guidance, protection, and love. You can recite traditional prayers such as "Omi Tutu," meaning "Mother River," as one of Oshun's domains is rivers. Alternatively, you can create your own prayers from the heart, whatever feels most authentic. It is important to focus on the intention of your prayer and speak from the heart to connect with Oshun's energy.

Honoring the goddess Oshun through prayer is an important aspect of spiritual practice. Here are a few suggestions for incorporating daily prayers and blessings into your routine:

Start each day with a prayer of gratitude to Oshun. Thank her for her guidance and blessings, and take a moment to appreciate and be grateful for all the positive things in your life. Expressing gratitude helps you to stay positive and open to receiving more blessings.

Before setting out for the day, offer a morning blessing to Oshun, asking for her protection and guidance throughout the day and for success in all your endeavors. This is also a great opportunity to set an intention or goal for the day.

At the end of each day, take some time to reflect on what has transpired during the day and offer an evening blessing to Oshun. You can use this moment to thank her for her guidance and protection and ask for her protection while you sleep.

Expressing creativity is another way to honor Oshun, as it involves opening yourself up emotionally, spiritually, and physically. When you feel inspired, create something unique, such as a painting, dance, or song, in honor of her presence in your life.

Lighting candles is an ancient practice used as a symbol of hope, faith, and guidance across many cultures, including the Yoruba people, who revere Oshun as one of their main deities. Sit quietly before lighting a candle dedicated solely to Oshun. Take a moment to breathe deeply and concentrate on her energy, letting go of any worries or troubles from the day. This can help to balance your emotions and bring inner peace and positive energy back into your life.

5. Spiritual Baths

A spiritual bath is a powerful and meaningful way to honor Oshun, the revered Orisha of beauty, love, and fertility. In the Yoruba tradition, taking a special bath with herbs and other natural ingredients is believed to purify the body and soul, honor Oshun, and attract her protection, blessings, and love into your life.

To truly connect with Oshun through a spiritual bath, it is important to engage all five senses: sight, smell, taste, touch, and sound. Start by setting an intention or prayer that acknowledges why you are connecting with her. Gather natural ingredients that have a symbolic meaning connected with Oshun, such as honey or cornmeal, which are known as "Sacred Waters" in Yoruba culture. Additionally, use herbs that correspond with Oshun, such as rose petals or lavender buds, to bring forth her soothing energy when ceremonially added to your water basin or tub.

If possible, take your spiritual bath near bodies of water, such as rivers, as water is closely tied to divinity in traditional African religions like Yoruba. Being in nature while taking your bath enhances the power of the cleansing ritual. Light candles around your bathroom basin or tub before beginning your ritual if this isn't possible. Singing is also a powerful addition; traditional Yoruba songs called Oriki that praise the Orishas can be used.

During the bath, focus on visualization and imagine yourself being surrounded by golden light, the color associated with Oshun, as it cleanses away any negative energy from your body and spirit. Once the bath is complete, reflect and allow the positive effects to sink deeply into your soul. As an offering, leave out a small token such as flowers or food outside near where you took a bath, giving back energy to nature.

6. Creativity

Honoring the Yoruba goddess Oshun through daily rituals and practices can bring peace, joy, and abundance into our lives. One powerful way to connect with Oshun is through prayer or meditation, where we offer gratitude and appreciation for her blessings and guidance.

Another way to honor Oshun is through creative expressions, such as painting, drawing, sculpting, or writing. Creating something to offer to Oshun can help focus your energy and provide a tangible representation of her presence in your life. Incorporating colors and symbols associated with Oshun, such as yellow, gold, orange, and symbols of water or rivers can further strengthen the connection with her energy.

Poetry is another way to honor Oshun daily. Writing about her attributes in poetic form can help bring her power into your own words and thoughts while focusing on specific areas that she governs, such as love or abundance, which can add even more meaning to your devotions.

Crafting candles, particularly yellow beeswax candles, can also be a powerful way to connect with Oshun. These candles can be used during prayer and meditation in her name and can also serve as an offering when accompanied by seeking blessings. Performance art, such as traditional African drumming, dancing, and singing, can also be used to honor Oshun, as it can elicit powerful responses from both the audience and the deity.

7. Practicing Self Love

Honoring Oshun, the Yoruba goddess of love, beauty, fertility, and abundance, can be done through daily practices which promote self-love and care. Here are some suggestions for how to honor Oshun in your daily life:

Speak kindly to yourself – As a goddess of love and compassion, Oshun wants you to treat yourself kindly. Speak words of encouragement and positivity to yourself each day to honor Oshun's nurturing nature. This will help you to cultivate greater self-esteem and confidence in yourself.

Take time for self-care – Taking time for yourself is a great way to honor Oshun and her divine femininity. Spend some time each day doing something pleasurable, such as reading a book or taking a warm bath. Doing something nice for yourself will help you feel better mentally and physically, allowing you to replenish your energy reserves so that you can be your best self for others throughout the day.

Avoid negative influences– Negative influences such as gossiping or judgmental people do not honor the spirit of Oshun's loving nature, so it is important to avoid them as much as possible to keep your energy positive. If you find yourself in situations where other people are being unkind or negative, take some deep breaths to ground yourself before you walk away from the situation to remain centered amidst any chaos around you.

Exercise mindfully – Practicing yoga, or another form of mindful movement, helps you to become aware of your body in space and helps you move past physical limitations you may have set upon yourself without even knowing it. Moving your body mindfully helps bring greater awareness into your life, which honors Oshun's devotion to beauty and artistry through movement.

Practice gratitude – Taking time daily to practice gratitude shifts your perspective from lack to abundance, which honors Oshun's symbolism for plenty. Keep a journal where you write down three things from your day that you are grateful for every night before bed.

Give back – One way to honor Oshun, the Yoruba goddess of love, beauty, fertility, and abundance, is through acts of generosity and giving back to others. By volunteering your time or resources to support a local non-profit organization or cause that aligns with your values, you can acknowledge and appreciate the abundance in your life and contribute to creating a more equitable and just world for all. This act of service not only honors Oshun's principles of compassion and generosity but also demonstrates your commitment to being a responsible steward of the blessings and resources you have been given.

Extra: Glossary of Terms

If you're new to African Traditional Religions, you've likely encountered several unfamiliar terms in this book. Use this glossary as your go-to guide if you need help understanding or remembering what any of the following terms mean.

Ajogun

The Ajogun is the personified form of evil forces. This personification manifests itself as 601 warriors who pursue warfare and battles to destroy humanity. There are 8 leaders of Ajogun: Ikú, the governor of death, Ègbà, the embodiment of paralysis; Òfò, the manifestation of loss; Èṣe, the essence of affliction; Èwọ̀n, the embodiment of imprisonment, Àrùn, the symbol of disease, Ọ̀ràn, the personified form of problems, and Èpè the symbol of curses.

Learn more about Ajogun in chapter 1.

Ashe

Ashe is a term that can reference three very important concepts in the Yoruba tradition. For one, it is used as an affirmation following a prayer. It is considered the equivalent of "Amen," and translates to "yes!" or "that's right!" Many natives even use it in informal contexts during their everyday lives. If you say something or share an idea with someone and they shout "Ashe," know that you said something they really like or agree with. This word is considered very affirming and expressive.

This word can also be used to refer to life energy or force. If you're interested in Indian or Chinese Traditional Medicine, you may find that the word "Ashe" is the equivalent of "Prana" or "Qi." People were all born with a specific amount of life force. Your experiences and choices in life, however, can either contribute to this amount or take away from it. Harmful, negative thoughts and toxic companies can decrease your life force, and the opposite is true. Yoruba practitioners believe that your Egún, or ancestors, are the ones who bless you with Ashe. They have created a certain grandeur and left it behind, so it becomes your Ashe. Yorubas also believe that descendants can contribute to your Ashe. Giving birth to them allows you to extend your bloodlines, which further expands your influence during your lifetime.

The last definition of Ashe is considered the most important and builds on the previous life force definition. It refers to the power that your words carry. Every word you speak carries the essence of Ashe since it's your life force. This is why Yorubas tie significant importance to and are very mindful of everything they say. They believe that you need to be very intentional about your words because you can manifest anything you say out loud. You want to be careful of what you attach your life force to.

When you hear something you deeply agree with, think about the role that your energy and existence play in the world or want to manifest an affirmation. End your sentence with "Ashe." Speak it with every bit of essence and life force energy you have.

Alternative spellings: Asé, Axé

Ashe is referenced in chapter 6.

Ataoja

Yoruba practitioners use the term Ataoja to refer to spiritual leaders or rulers. The term translates to "the person who can drink water from a fish's mouth." Being a spiritual leader, the Ataoja is expected to offer blessings to the public and practice spiritual healing. Some people believe that the Ataoja garners their strength from the river and uses this power to help their people during times of need.

Ataoja is mentioned in chapter 9.

Ayanmo

Ayanmo, which means destiny or fate, is a very important concept in African Traditional Religions. This term describes a person's spiritual intentions or will, the future, and the force that controls all events. According to Yoruba beliefs, a person's environment, date of birth, and the present moment all shape their Ayanmo. It is also believed that a person chooses their Ayanmo upon their birth.

Learn more about Ayanmo in chapter 1.

Babalawo

The term Babalawo, also known as Babaaláwo, translates to "the father of hidden secrets/mysteries." This highly esteemed title describes the Ifá oracle's high priest.

Babalawo is mentioned in chapter 2.

Ifá

Ifá is a divination system that represents the teachings of the Òrìsà Orunmila, the Òrìsà of Wisdom, who in turn serves as the oracular representative of Olodumare.

Learn more about Ifá in chapter 1.

Ile Ife

According to Yorubas, Ile Ife is where their civilization first came to life. They also believe that the gods stayed in this city when they traveled to Earth. The city's name translates to "place or location of dispersion." They say that the Orishas Obatala and Oduduwa were the ones who founded this city when they were creating the world. The Yoruba tradition suggests that Oduduwa appointed himself as the first Yoruban king, while Oduduwa created the world's first citizens using clay.

However, historically speaking, the Igbo people were already inhabitants of the area that later became known as Yorubaland when Oduduwa arrived. His army approached the city's northern borders, pushing the Igbos out and to the east. When Oduduwa died, his descendants started expanding Yorubaland and founded new cities surrounding Ile Ife. It was not long before Yoruba became one of the largest ethnic groups on the continent.

Find out more about the celebrations that take place in Ile Ife in chapter 9.

Kariocha

Kariocha, otherwise known as "making ocha," is the initiation process of a new priest or priestess that is a part of the Santería Lukumi African Traditional Religion. During this week-long ceremony, a person's tutelary, Orisha, is crowned on their head. The initiate then enters a year and 7 days long period known as Iyaworaje, during which they experience purification, rebirth, and transformation and expand their knowledge.

Kariocha and making ocha are mentioned in chapter 2.

Omi Tutu

Prayers and offering liberations are two crucial aspects of Ifá Orisha rituals. Practitioners are expected to do both regardless of how simple and intricate the ritual they're conducting is. Libations are completed in the form of Oriki – the act of praise. Performing Oriki is a means of acknowledging the energy of the Orisha while asking them for their guidance and blessings. According to practitioners, these prayers and rituals promote the opening of the consciousness of those who perform them. This can be valuable in any ceremony, ritual, or other spiritual endeavors because it aids in aligning their consciousness with that of the divine forces, making it easier to contact them.

Omi Tutu is a traditional prayer that practitioners use to invoke divine forces to bring cooling energy to the practitioner. It's also used as an enhancement prayer - practitioners use it to manifest anything they want through ancestral intervention. Omi Tutu is usually recited at the beginning of any ritual before partaking in any spiritual practices. A cool water libation is often offered to the Orisha when reciting the prayer. This prayer is also popularly used in spiritual cleansing rituals because it removes negative energy and makes the practitioner more receptive to the guidance of Orisha.

Learn more about prayers and when to use Omi Tutu in chapter 10.

Ori

The Ori is an African traditional metaphysical idea. The word literally translates to "head" but often points at an individual's Ayanmo (destiny) and intuition. The Ori is the embodiment of the human consciousness, which is why several belief systems regard it as an Orisha on its own. Some practitioners worship their Ori, appease it through offerings, and pray to it just as they would for any other Orisha. It's believed that working with your Ori can help you lead a more harmonious life and enhance your character. Practitioners often ask Ori for guidance whenever they're experiencing challenges because they believe that Ori is responsible for everything that happens in a person's life - it determines one's destiny.

Mentioned in chapter 2.

Orisha

An Orisha is one of the deities (plural: Orishas) in the pantheon worshipped by several African peoples - most notably, the Yorubas of southwestern Nigeria. The Ewe peoples of Benin, Ghana, and Togo, the Edo peoples of southeastern Nigeria, and the Fon of Benin also venerate the Orishas. While the myths and rituals associated with the Orishas might differ from place to place, the underlying spiritual concepts of all Traditional African Religions are relatively similar. Some people claim that the definition of "deity" doesn't capture the real essence of the Orisha and suggest that it is an intricate, multidimensional unifying force.

Alternative spellings: orixa, orisa

Tutelary Orisha

Every person has a tutelary or head Orisha. This entity is also popularly known as a guardian Orisha because they serve as your spiritual guides and for balancing life forces. They are called head Orishas because they claim the individual's head once they are acknowledged. Knowing and working with your tutelary Orisha is a lifelong commitment. Practitioners don't get to choose their head Orishas - they're determined by a person's destiny at birth. You can only attain your Ayanmo if you follow the guidance of this force. According to the Santería Lukumi belief system, only 9 Orishas can serve as tutelary Orishas.

See chapter 2 to learn more about tutelary Orishas.

Conclusion

Oshun is the youngest of the Orishas and is often considered the gentlest one. She is the patron of the rivers, love, and sensuality. She is also associated with fertility and new beginnings. However, despite her seemingly serene and benevolent nature, she is one of the most empowering female forces you can seek out. She is patient and not easily angered, but like all Yoruba deities, she has negative aspects too. Oshun is known to be a vain creature, often displaying jealousy and acting in spite. Ruling over rivers, she can easily take away the life her waters gave by flooding the fruitful lands.

Oshun is central to the ancient Yoruba religion, and Santeria and Ifa - and each of these belief systems have tales and myths associated with her. One of the most famous ones revolves around Oshun's contribution to the population of Earth - only rivaled by her love story with Shango, the mighty thunder god. According to the Yoruba myths, humanity only exists because of Oshun, the goddess of love and fertility. She is the mother of many; if you're attracted to her power, she may be your Orisha parent too. If this is the case, the information you've gained by reading this book will be an excellent stepping stone for building a substantial relationship with her.

The goddess Oshun is the universal archetype of the divine feminine, an incredibly potent and spiritually uplifting source of female power. Connecting with this aspect of Oshun (as well as with any other ones) is only possible after learning correspondence and favorite offerings. For example, knowing that she prefers to receive offerings and be addressed near running or sweet waters can help you appease her and ask for her favors and blessings. Similarly, representing her with the colors gold and yellow and the multitude of natural elements linked to her will allow you to form a powerful bond with her.

Oshun is often called on by women who struggle with infertility, but she can also bring productivity into any area of your life. You can also request her assistance when struggling financially or when you wish to empower yourself through sensuality. You can work with her at her favorite places or dedicate an altar to her. The latter is particularly beneficial for daily practices and for many other reasons related to spirituality, magic, and self-empowerment. Besides working with her, the spells and rituals contained in this book will aid your spiritual growth and help you become a more confident and self-loving version of yourself.

Oshun is typically venerated on Fridays, as this is her favorite day. She is also celebrated through several festivals held by the devotees of Yoruba and African Diaspora religions. One of the most popular events is the Osun Osogbo festival, held during the last week of August. This momentous event celebrates several other Yoruba deities, culminating with elaborate rituals held in Oshun's honor. Another great way to honor the goddess of love is through daily self-care rituals, such as meditation, journaling, singing, baths, and more. You can use the ones referenced in this book or devise a pampering ritual of your own. Either way, the goal is to become empowered and ready to take on any challenge in love or any other aspect of your life.

Here's another book by Mari Silva that you might like

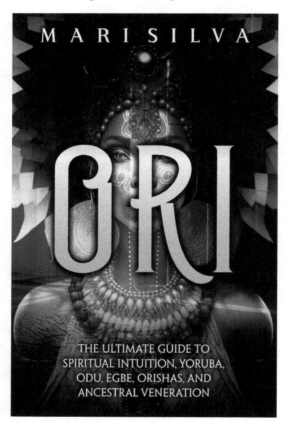

Your Free Gift
(only available for a limited time)

Thanks for getting this book! If you want to learn more about various spirituality topics, then join Mari Silva's community and get a free guided meditation MP3 for awakening your third eye. This guided meditation mp3 is designed to open and strengthen ones third eye so you can experience a higher state of consciousness. Simply visit the link below the image to get started.

https://spiritualityspot.com/meditation

References

31 Days of Revolutionary Women, #16: Oshun. (2017, March 16). South Seattle Emerald. https://southseattleemerald.com/2017/03/16/31-days-of-revolutionary-women-16-oshun/

Baltimore Sun - We are currently unavailable in your region. (n.d.). Baltimoresun.com. https://www.baltimoresun.com/maryland/bs-md-african-faiths-20190315-story.html

Beyer, C. (2012, June 14). The Orishas: Orunla, Osain, Oshun, Oya, and Yemaya. Learn Religions. https://www.learnreligions.com/orunla-osain-oshun-oya-and-yemaya-95923

Brandon, G. (2018). orisha. In Encyclopedia Britannica.

Cuban Santeria tradition and practices. (n.d.). Anywhere.com. https://www.anywhere.com/cuba/travel-guide/santeria

Imoka, A. (2019, April 11). Who is Oshun Santeria? El Viejo Lazaro. https://www.viejolazaro.com/blogs/news/who-is-oshun-santeria

Imoka-Ubochioma, C. (2021, December 8). The Yoruba story of creation. Linkedin.com. https://www.linkedin.com/pulse/yoruba-story-creation-dr-chizoba-imoka-ubochioma/

Jeffries, B. S. (2022). Oshun. In Encyclopedia Britannica.

Mark, J. J. (2021b). Oshun. World History Encyclopedia. https://www.worldhistory.org/Oshun/

Mesa, V. (2018, April 20). How to invoke Oshun, the Yoruba goddess of sensuality and prosperity. VICE. https://www.vice.com/en/article/3kjepv/how-to-invoke-oshun-yoruba-goddess-orisha

Murphy, J. M. (2022). Santería. In Encyclopedia Britannica.

Ochún. (n.d.). AboutSanteria. http://www.aboutsanteria.com/ochuacuten.html

Oshun - Yoruba deity and goddess of the river. (n.d.). Realmermaids.net. http://www.realmermaids.net/mermaid-legends/oshun/

What is Santeria? (n.d.). AboutSanteria. http://www.aboutsanteria.com/what-is-santeria.html

Wigington, P. (2011, November 15). What is the Santeria religion? Learn Religions. https://www.learnreligions.com/about-santeria-traditions-2562543

Wigington, P. (2019, November 29). Yoruba religion: History and beliefs. Learn Religions. https://www.learnreligions.com/yoruba-religion-4777660

Yoruba. (n.d.). Everyculture.com. https://www.everyculture.com/wc/Mauritania-to-Nigeria/Yoruba.html

Children of Oshun – see the characteristics and find out if you are one of them! (2022, September 27). Love Magic Works. https://lovemagicworks.com/children-of-oshun-see-the-characteristics-and-find-out-if-you-are-one-of-them/

Church, S. (n.d.). The head or guardian, Orisha. Santeria Church of the Orishas. http://santeriachurch.org/head-or-guardian-orisha/

Oshun: The Yoruban goddess of love. (2013, March 18). The Broom Closet. https://broomcloset.wordpress.com/2013/03/19/oshun-the-yoruban-goddess-of-love/

Rogers, M. R. (2022, July 6). How to find your Orisha mother and father? Classified Mom. https://www.classifiedmom.com/how-to-find-your-orisha-mother-and-father/

Terrio, S. J. (2019). Whose child, am I?: Unaccompanied, undocumented children in U.s. immigration custody. University of California Press. https://doi.org/10.1525/9780520961449

Abisoye. (2021, August 13). The mythological powers of Oba's ears. Plus, TV Africa. https://plustvafrica.com/the-mythological-powers-of-obas-ears/

Amarachi. (2017, December 10). Orisha: The Legend of Sango & his Wives. Travel with a Pen Nigerian Travel Blog. https://www.travelwithapen.com/orisha-legend-sango-wives/

Celebrate obatalá, the Orisha who made the world and people. (2022, September 26). New York Latin Culture Magazine TM; New York Latin Culture Magazine. https://www.newyorklatinculture.com/obatala/

Control of the seasons in the new kingdom - The Yoruba Religious Concepts. (n.d.). Google.com. https://sites.google.com/site/theyorubareligiousconcepts/control-of-the-seasons-in-the-new-kingdom

Nut_Meg, O. (n.d.). Oshun. Obsidianportal.com. https://god-touched.obsidianportal.com/characters/oshun-1

Ochún. (n.d.). AboutSanteria. http://www.aboutsanteria.com/ochuacuten.html

Oshun loses her beauty. (n.d.). Uua.org. https://www.uua.org/re/tapestry/children/signs/session13/oshun

Prince_miraj. (n.d.). How oshun lured ogun from the forest. Wattpad.com. https://www.wattpad.com/522478079-nigerian-tribe-myth%27s-african-how-oshun-lured-ogun

Roy, M. (2020, May 7). Eshu, Yoruba trickster god. Minute Mythology. https://medium.com/minute-mythology/eshu-yoruba-trickster-god-a09fd22ca48c

Santos, E. (2020). Oxum. Solisluna Editora.

The birth of Oshun ibu yumu - the Yoruba Religious concepts. (n.d.). Google.com. https://sites.google.com/site/theyorubareligiousconcepts/the-birth-of-oshun-ibu-yumu-1

The Editors of Encyclopedia Britannica. (2015). Eshu. In Encyclopedia Britannica.

Wikipedia contributors. (2022, December 22). Aganju. Wikipedia, The Free Encyclopedia. https://en.wikipedia.org/w/index.php?title=Aganju&oldid=1128829112

Yemaya abandons Arganyu in Oshuns Ile - The Yoruba Religious Concepts. (n.d.). Google.com. https://sites.google.com/site/theyorubareligiousconcepts/yemaya-abandons-arganyu-in-oshuns-ile

Yemaya offers Oshun marriage with Arganyu - The Yoruba Religious Concepts. (n.d.). Google.com. https://sites.google.com/site/theyorubareligiousconcepts/yemaya-offers-oshun-marriage-with-arganyu

Aletheia. (2018, March 4). Divine Masculine: 9 ways to awaken your inner Shiva ★ LonerWolf. LonerWolf.

Anusara School of Hatha Yoga. (2022, August 28). 6 easy ways to connect with the divine feminine. Anusara School of Hatha Yoga. https://www.anusarayoga.com/6-easy-ways-to-connect-with-divine-feminine/

Davis, F. (2021, October 8). How to embody your divine feminine qualities. Karma and Luck. https://www.karmaandluck.com/blogs/news/divine-feminine-qualities

Divine Feminine: Meaning, origins, and more. (n.d.). Tiny Rituals. https://tinyrituals.co/blogs/tiny-rituals/divine-feminine

Tiodar, A. (2021, June 1). 11 amazing qualities of the Divine Feminine explained. Subconscious Servant. https://subconsciousservant.com/divine-feminine-qualities/

What the "divine feminine" is all about & 9 ways anyone can embody it. (2021, March 22). Mindbodygreen. https://www.mindbodygreen.com/articles/divine-feminine

Rodríguez, C. (2020, August 23). 10 representative plants of Oshún. Ashé pa mi Cuba. https://ashepamicuba.com/en/plantas-de-oshun/

Goddess Oshun. (2012, January 21). Journeying to the Goddess. https://journeyingtothegoddess.wordpress.com/2012/01/21/goddess-oshun/

My Yoruba. (n.d.). Tumblr. https://myoruba.tumblr.com/post/82996905534/oshuns-herbs

Rhys, D. (2022, November 6). Oshun – Symbolism of the Yoruba Goddess. Symbol Sage. https://symbolsage.com/african-goddess-of-love/

Kaufman, A. (2022, October 31). Oshun Offerings: What are the Offerings to Oshun to Ask for Help? Digest From Experts. https://digestfromexperts.com/4516/oshun-offerings/

Universe, V. (2014, September 8). Oshun's Butternut Squash Soup Recipe. Voodoo Universe. https://www.patheos.com/blogs/voodoouniverse/2014/09/oshuns-butternut-squash-soup-recipe/

View all posts by Simone Soulel Co. (2019, September 10). Oshun's Feast Day Recipes: Honey Yams ! The Bruja Encyclopedia. https://coven90210.wordpress.com/2019/09/10/oshuns-feast-day-recipes-honey-yams/

Scott-James, N. (2020, October 30). Ori Ye Ye O: Honoring the Yoruba Goddess Oshun. The Alchemist's Kitchen. https://wisdom.thealchemistskitchen.com/ori-ye-ye-o-yoruba-goddess-oshun/

Siren Says. (2009, May 11). Siren Says. https://sirensays.wordpress.com/2009/05/11/oshun-altar/

How to Invoke the Energy of Yorube Goddess Oshun. (2018, April 20). Vice.Com. https://www.vice.com/en/article/3kjepv/how-to-invoke-oshun-yoruba-goddess-orisha

Urošević, A. (2015, September 23). Spiritual Cleansing in Ifá: "Sour" and "Sweet" Baths. Amor et Mortem. https://amoretmortem.wordpress.com/2015/09/23/spiritual-cleansing-in-ifa-sour-and-sweet-baths/

Lousfey, D. (n.d.). Love Spells. SHUBHAM

Oshun Ritual with Yeye Luisah Teish for Love and Prosperity presented by the Neighborhood Story Project. (n.d.). P.5 Yesterday We Said Tomorrow. https://www.prospect5.org/programs/pp46cnl2n50rmcbjegutylqka9e4tx

Botanica, Y. [@YeyeoBotanica]. (2019, August 29). Oshun Fertility Ritual | Yeyeo Botanica. Youtube. https://www.youtube.com/watch?v=RFAZQSWRIp4

Botanica, Y. [@YeyeoBotanica]. (2017, January 30). Oshun Protection & Special Request | Yeyeo Botanica. Youtube. https://www.youtube.com/watch?v=RFAZQSWRIp4

No title. (n.d.). Twinkl.Co.In. https://www.twinkl.co.in/event/osun-festival-nigeria-2023

Rankin, L. M. (2019, July 3). A goddess for giving and receiving love. Human Parts. https://humanparts.medium.com/a-goddess-for-giving-and-receiving-love-7541cb73ad65

Sacred journeys with Bruce feiler. (n.d.). SACRED JOURNEYS WITH BRUCE FEILER. https://www.pbs.org/wgbh/sacredjourneys/content/osun-osogbo/

Regla De Ocha, ■., Candomble, ■., Lucumi, ■., Oyo, ■., Palo, ■., Palo, M. ■., Santeria, M. ■., & Ifa, Y. ■. (n.d.). ■ Regla de Ocha Candomble Lucumi Oyo Palo Mayumbe Palo Monte Santeria Vodun Yoruba Ifa Religious Practices. Bop.gov. https://www.bop.gov/foia/docs/orishamanual.pdf

Top 10 oshun prayer ideas and inspiration. (n.d.). Pinterest. https://www.pinterest.com/ideas/oshun-prayer/899688434063/

About: Babalawo. (n.d.). DBpedia. https://dbpedia.org/page/Babalawo

About: Ori (Yoruba). (n.d.). DBpedia. https://dbpedia.org/page/Ori_(Yoruba)

Ajogun. (n.d.). Wiktionary.org. https://en.wiktionary.org/wiki/Ajogun

Alamy Limited. (n.d.). Osun Osogbo Monarch: Ataoja of Osogbo wearing his sacred crown on Osun Day. Alamy.com. https://www.alamy.com/osun-osogbo-monarch-ataoja-of-osogbo-wearing-his-sacred-crown-on-osun-day-image425916626.html

Dopamu, A. (2008). Predestination, destiny, and faith in Yorubaland: Any meeting point? Global Journal of Humanities, 7(1 & 2), 37–39. https://www.ajol.info/index.php/gjh/article/view/79372

Facebook. (n.d.). Facebook.com. https://web.facebook.com/StJohnsSpiritualBaptistChurch/posts/omi-tutu-that-is-water-that-calmsthis-ritual-is-very-oldthere-are-many-reasons-f/1874345729265590/?_rdc=1&_rdr

LibGuides: African Traditional Religions: Ifa: Chapter 5: Our ancestors are with us now. (2021). https://atla.libguides.com/c.php?g=1138564&p=8384925

Recio, S. (2019, February 14). What have I done? And other answers to your questions —. Sili Recio. https://silirecio.com/blog/what-have-i-done-and-other-answers-to-your-questions

The Ataoja of Osogbo land. (n.d.). Google Arts & Culture. https://artsandculture.google.com/asset/the-ataoja-of-osogbo-land/JwEH7uuwlNpEeQ?hl=en

The Spiritual Attorney. (2019, September 24). Ase': What it is & why it's important. TheSpiritualAttorney. https://www.thespiritualattorney.com/post/manage-your-blog-from-your-live-site

(N.d.). Blackpast.org. https://www.blackpast.org/global-african-history/ile-ife-ca-500-b-c-e/

(2019, December 25). Oshun: African Goddess of Love and Sweet Waters. Ancient Origins Reconstructing the Story of Humanity's Past; Ancient Origins. https://www.ancient-origins.net/myths-legends-africa/oshun-african-goddess-love-and-sweet-waters-002908